"Dara Baldwin is courageous, committed, the definition of intersectional, and a fierce movement builder. We can learn much from her."

—V (FORMERLY EVE ENSLER), author of
The Vagina Monologues and *Reckoning*

"*To Be a Problem* is a revolutionary text from a unique perspective all too ignored in our society. In a time when dehumanization is on the march, to read a book so rooted in our collective humanity is an absolute gift. Dara Baldwin is a special writer, as anyone who reads these pages will find out for themselves."

—DAVE ZIRIN, author of *The Kaepernick Effect*
and sports editor of *The Nation*

"Dara Baldwin is a visionary organizer who applies her razor-sharp intellect to the task of building movements that include the most marginalized, not as an afterthought but as the only possible route to winning the world we need. This book is a badly needed intervention in our times of overlapping and intersecting crises."

—NAOMI KLEIN, author of
The Shock Doctrine and *Doppelganger*

"Discover the remarkable journey of Dara Baldwin in her manifesto, where she fearlessly challenges the disability rights movement, advocating for disability justice and amplifying the voices of disabled BIPOC. Her passionate call for change will leave you inspired to champion a more inclusive and equitable world."

—BRITTANY K. BARNETT, author of
A Knock at Midnight

"Baldwin makes plain that the Americans with Disabilities Act is about more than doors and ramps. It is the minimum required to build a truly inclusive society where we all participate. If you want to understand what disability justice, solidarity, and intersectionality are, and if you want to know how to show up in the movement for an inclusive multiracial democracy, read this book."

—ZACH NORRIS, author of *Defund Fear:
Safety Without Policing, Prisons, and Punishment*

"Dara Baldwin is an incredibly dynamic leader who embodies the true meaning of solidarity and understands intersectionality better than almost anyone. Dara's voice, and this book, is so unique and critical in this moment."

—SARU JAYARAMAN, president of One Fair Wage

"As spirited an author as she is an activist, Dara Baldwin brings tenacity, passion, and an intimate insight into the racial landscape of the disability rights movement. *To Be a Problem* not only demystifies the notion of a monolithic movement for disability rights but brings to clarity how the overlapping intersections of race and racism, Blackness and gender, leave many disabled individuals stuck at the margins, invisible, and silenced. This book reads like a freedom song for these overlooked segments of the disability rights movement(s), with Dara Baldwin crafting lyrics that speak hope and courage to readers."

—KHALED A. BEYDOUN, law professor
and author of *American Islamophobia*

"I would regularly see Dara Baldwin in the halls of Congress as she did the hard work of lobbying for disability rights. Her frustration was not just with Congress but also with her own disability movement, which she found to be racist, insulting, and oppressive. Her hard-hitting exposé will hopefully lead to reflection and transformation, not only in that movement but in all of our movements that continue to be plagued by elitism and white privilege."

—MEDEA BENJAMIN, peace activist
and cofounder of CODEPINK

"From Dara Baldwin's powerful storytelling in this book, one learns about history that is far too often white-washed, leaving out the powerful contributions of Black women including Lois Curtis and the roles of key figures such as Asian American advocate Yoshiko Dart. Baldwin also clearly names the problematic tendency to compare disparate historical moments across our identities that falsely equate our nation's history with enslaving Black people with its failures to provide access to disabled people. Baldwin provides example after example of how she has spoken truth to power, educated others, and persisted through problematic and hurtful experiences as a DC activist and lobbyist for disability justice. This book is a testament to Baldwin's family, faith, courage, and the many times she has brought race into necessary rooms through her presence and through naming things that are far too often unsaid, in the hope of creating more authentic movements by and for those of us who are multi-marginalized."

—SUNU P. CHANDY, civil rights attorney
and author of *My Dear Comrades*

"Dara Baldwin's *To Be a Problem* is an incisive book that helps build necessary connections between all of our movements with the disability rights movements. Clear and filled with purpose, Dara's voice cuts to the heart of what needs to change while also opening a pathway to how Black feminists like Dara are the foundation of the solution. Her commitment to intersectional col-liberation rings true, and this book is a wonderful addition to the library of all changemakers."

—THENMOZHI SOUNDARARAJAN,
author of *The Trauma of Caste: A Dalit Feminist Meditation on Survivorship, Healing, and Abolition*

"Dara Baldwin is a movement warrior for justice. She is an insistent voice for those with disabilities, seeing the connection with all other struggles for justice and freedom and democracy. She comforts the afflicted and afflicts the comfortable—she is a problem for those who cause problems for others, in order to make this a more just world."

—HEATHER BOOTH, American civil rights activist

"Dara Baldwin writes, as she says, from a place of 'frustration, anger, and continued recovery,' but she acts out of love for the collective liberation of all. A tireless disrupter who wears her scars proudly, she knows that movements steeped in whiteness will not get us where we need to go."

—LAURA FLANDERS, author and
host of *The Laura Flanders Show*

"What do you do if you are a Black female committed to a full and meaningful life for everyone, especially including BIPOC disabled people? You write this book that indicts the ableism, prejudice, and bigotry of the existing disability rights movement. Dara gives visibility to the multi-marginalized communities of the disabled. She condemns covert disenfranchisement. She reveals the caste status of being born disabled in a country of the 'survival of the fittest.' She uncovers the problem and points to its resolution: BIPOC disabled people need to be at the heart of disability justice. Black liberation and abolitionism become the new promise of full citizenship for abled and disabled alike."

—ZILLAH EISENSTEIN, activist and
author of *Abolitionist Socialist Feminism*

TO BE A PROBLEM

A BLACK WOMAN'S SURVIVAL IN THE RACIST DISABILITY RIGHTS MOVEMENT

DARA BALDWIN

BEACON PRESS, BOSTON

BEACON PRESS
Boston, Massachusetts
www.beacon.org

Beacon Press books
are published under the auspices of
the Unitarian Universalist Association of Congregations.

27 26 25 24   8 7 6 5 4 3 2 1

This book is printed on acid-free paper that meets the uncoated
paper ANSI/NISO specifications for permanence as revised in 1992.

Text design and composition by Kim Arney

*Library of Congress Cataloging-in-Publication
Data is available for this title.*
ISBN: 978-0-8070-1397-7
E-book: 978-0-8070-1398-4
audiobook: 978-0-8070-0371-8
large print: 978-0-8070-1738-8

Dedicated to my mother,
Lillian Lula Baldwin,
my angel forever
protecting me

CONTENTS

FOREWORD

As a person of color with a disability who has been in the disability race movement for well over three decades, I can tell you that there are things in this book that you will discover are true. There are rankings within our disability community as to, quote, preferred disabilities, unquote. In my career early on, there was a discussion about cross-disability, cross-cultural outreach for people with disabilities who were Black, who were Laotian, Hispanic, or Latinx, or First Nation and Indigenous, and how the movement seemed to have passed them by.

What you will find in Dara's book is a perspective and a truth that are often overlooked and ignored about our very movement or movements. Social justice has become not only about movement but is also an industry that excludes individuals with disabilities. It excludes women of color from moving up and presenting and fighting for those things that we know affect all our communities.

We also understand that, within this movement, there are those who are lauded as icons, giants of the movement, those who are seen as the thought leaders and thinkers where positionality has shifted them from fighting for justice to preserving their position. It is outstanding to have someone take the courage to write what most of the community knows to be true.

But in my career, there have been times in which I've chosen to ignore the racism, to ignore the classism, to ignore what we know to be toxic behavior for the greater good. This has reared its head in policy meetings and when engaging in other situations in which we are fighting for social justice.

However, even with that, there is still a distinction when you add the fact of being a woman of color in this movement. So what you will take away from this book, I hope, is that people are people regardless if they are disabled or not, but behaviors are still detrimental to the cause in which we are all seeking to be fulfilled. That is for our humanity to be embraced, respected, and for us to have the ability to live our lives as we see fit.

Again, I commend Dara Baldwin for such a brave and powerful book. It is amazing that we are at a place where people still don't believe that it happens. But by the end of this, you will understand the pitfalls and the trappings that come along with fighting for social justice inside a movement that has yet to reconcile itself with those things.

—KEITH P. JONES, disability justice activist

INTRODUCTION

I come from a beautiful, caring, strong, and courageous people who are from the amazing continent of Africa. Every day I am surrounded by my ancestorial angels who cover me in grace and love. The following pages are in my words about my story of working and surviving in the racist supremacist disability rights community as a nondisabled Black activist. All too often Black people's stories are stolen, co-opted, reconfigured, ignored, challenged, and/or invalidated to make white people feel comfortable. As I wrote this book, this is the movement that is currently happening throughout the world but especially in the United States. Eliminating the true stories of the foundations of this country is part of the modus operandi for conservative and progressive white people, a truth many suppress and block from conversations about what is truly happening.

In the summer of 2018, I decided to write about working in the problematic disability rights community. It has been a mission of love because I was raised by a strong Black woman named Lillian Baldwin, who taught me to "never change you" and to "embrace your greatness with humility."

I have been blessed to know many authors, and it was their love and care that guided me to scribe my story with the intent of creating change. The tides of fate offered me this opportunity to tell this ugly truth about my traumatic experience with the power to include hope and love for the future. It is an honor to work with so many people outside the racist disability rights community, who have shown me that there is a future for Black liberation that includes abolitionism and collective liberation.

Rev. Dr. Martin Luther King Jr. discussed power and said, "Power without love is reckless and abusive and . . . love without power is sentimental and anemic. Power at its best is love implementing the demands of justice. Justice at its best is love correcting everything that stands against love."[1] In the disability rights movement they are quick to quote MLK Jr. But they are not quick to accept that their power within the movement is reckless and abusive. They also do not accept that the implementing demands for justice, by BIPOC and multi-marginalized disabled people, are not only ignored but even ridiculed, which in no way encompasses love.

One of my many blessings has been to work in social justice activism for most of my life. I did this as a layperson because I was the daughter of a member of Delta Sigma Theta Sorority, Inc., and in a family who worshipped in the AME (African Methodist Episcopal) Church. Both are entities with a foundation that is submerged in the social justice movement around the globe. My professional life as an activist and policy analyst started in 2004 with the completion of my master's degree in public administration from Rutgers University. I worked for almost twenty years in corporate America with overt racism before entering the social justice profession in 2004. This work is mostly done through the nonprofit industrial complex. I thought this was a different and maybe even safe space for Black excellence, a place where "progressive and liberal" white people are the dominant leaders doing things differently. But I soon learned that in every industrial complex system, white supremacy and racism reign supreme. The treatment of Black people in social justice work and in particular the disability rights movement is appalling.

The title of this book comes from the brilliant prose of *The Souls of Black Folk* by W. E. B. Du Bois, where he discusses the white Southerners who questioned the existence of being Black. The section is about Du Bois responding *"To the real question, How does it feel to be a problem?"* in the United States. This indirect offensive question about the Black body actually "being a problem" holds precious knowledge for this Black activist. I learned early in my work within the disability rights movement that my very existence in a room was a problem. My ability to analyze the racist policy agendas was a problem. My understanding of the white supremacy and privilege that permeate almost every event and the outreach of this movement was a problem. Every group has problems, but it will not tolerate a problem that can disrupt and dismantle the systems of power. In my case this manifested into a horrible work environment.

This book is my story as the only person of color to work on a policy level in one of the largest disability coalitions in the country, with over one hundred organizations, for over ten years. Note that I say "person of color," not just Black, because, believe it or not, there was no representation of Asian American, Latina, or Indigenous people in policy positions. There are few people with visible disabilities who are policy staffers and only about seven women in positions of leadership. Yes, these statistics are as of 2022.

It is also my declaration to the thousands of Black, Indigenous, People of Color (BIPOC) who are disabled that there is no need to wait for the disability rights community to "get it together" or to change. Not with the creation of disability justice, which is a new and powerful movement that focuses on BIPOC disabled people. And the work being done around the world to enhance and create change for BIPOC disabled people must be at the center of all social justice work. It is time for the social justice movement to embrace the fact that if we dismantle the systemic problems and barriers of BIPOC disabled people, then we will create the new world order that is collective liberation for all.

I write this from a place of frustration, anger, and continued recovery from the trauma of dealing with microaggressions and racial harassment in public policy in the national disability rights movement based in Washington, DC.

The disability rights community embraces covert racism. They refuse to reprimand or rebuke anyone in the community who has been blatantly racist or chose those they don't like and ridicule them. But if they are in good with the larger community, nothing is said to these horrible people. There is an actual nickname for this crew; they are called "the disability mafia."

It is a community that has perpetuated racism while suppressing those facing discrimination. In their disingenuous promises to make a difference, they continue to dominate the conversation and prevent any change in their advocacy faction by keeping it an all-white one. They preserve their dominance by telling those in this community who are oppressed that they are overly sensitive, angry, confrontational, and disrespectful, and are overreacting, which is an intentional use of their majority to perpetuate suppression. I hope to inspire others who are striving valiantly to reverse the harms that continue to be inflicted in this space. My desire is to give hope to every person who works tirelessly to end the trauma caused in this space.

This conversation about the toxic workplace environment in the nonprofit world has been suppressed by many. This is not a phenomenon of white-led organizations, as many BIPOC leaders and Black leaders have been accused of engaging in harmful employment spaces as well. So much so that many of our nation's leading social justice organizations' staffs have had to unionize in order to be treated fairly and paid fair wages for their work. Imagine working for an organization that fights for fair pay and fair treatment in the workplace, for the country, and is not providing these things for their own staff. This is happening in DC and around the country right now.

The pages of this book are written about my tortured experiences. It infuriates me to have to write this story in 2023, but it's my experience and I feel it should be shared. It begins with a description of who I am, because after almost every presentation I do, the first set of questions is "Who are you? And how did you come to do this work?" Sometimes they are asked out of pure curiosity, but most times they come out of frustration and anger because I have been a truth teller about white people, which causes them discomfort and fear.

The story moves on to discuss my fifteen-plus-year career in the disability rights movement. I discuss overt and covert racism; the reason white supremacy continues to reign in this movement and why a completely new movement, disability justice, was created to counter this work; and how harmful the disability rights movement is to all social justice work; and I finish with a discussion on where there is hope and recommendations for crafting change for the work of creating a new world order through the leadership of the BIPOC disabled community. In this work I am always up-front and honest about not being a person with a disability, yet after about five years into my work, because I was in solidarity with disabled people, many told me "you are part of the family." It is the same label I get from my LGBTQIA+ family. To be genuine in solidarity means credibility and acceptance.

Writing this book has been a journey of love for my people, filled with many emotions from disappointment to exhilaration. This is but a piece of my life, the part where I engaged with a harmful movement. It does not define me and there is much more to be told. I hope all who read this find it informational, useful, and hopeful. I chose to write about my experiences during this part of my life not only for myself but for the thousands of Black activists and staff working in and around these toxic social justice organizations, and especially for those who try or have given up trying to work in the disability rights community.

Before we begin, it's important to note that language matters and having some mutual understanding about how various terms are used is important. These words/terms are used in social justice work, and over the years I have seen them be torn apart, co-opted, and used by many white advocates mostly, in their work to create change. But the origins of these words largely come from Black activists who knew and currently know what they are talking about when they are used. Yet our thoughts about these words are constantly obscured, rearranged, and harmed to protect the feelings of white advocates, so it's important to reclaim them. Here I provide explanations of commonly misunderstood terms through the lens of disability justice.

Activist/s—A person/people who engages in intentional actions to bring about social or political change. This is the disability justice movement.

Advocate/s—A person/people who works on behalf of a person, group, or organization. The disability rights movement in DC is dominated by this group, which is mostly made up of cisgender, upper-middle-class, nondisabled white women.

Caste apartheid is a structure of oppression that affects over one billion people across the world. It is a system of religiously codified exclusion that was established in Hindu scripture. At birth, every child inherits his or her ancestors' caste, which determines social status and assigns "spiritual purity."[2]

Collective liberation is the work of liberating all multi-marginalized people from the multiple forms of economic, political, religious, and social subjugation with a concise focus on creating a world that leaves no one behind. This is used in disability justice movement work.

Comparative suffering is trying to make sense of one group's pain by comparing it to another group's pain or, in the disability rights movement, comparing their type of plight to those of significance to Black communities, i.e., when comparing and describing the deinstitutionalization of disabled people as the Disability Underground Railroad. Disability rights people strongly believe that there are "similarities and overlap" to the incomparable Harriet Tubman's Underground Railroad and the work she did freeing enslaved Black people in the US.

Disability, as defined in the Americans with Disabilities Act (ADA) of 1990, is a physical or mental impairment that substantially limits one or more major life activities. This law applies to people from cradle to death. Many do not use or think the ADA is for children and youth. This is a disservice to that community.

Disability justice is a social justice movement that focuses on examining disability and ableism as they relate to other forms of oppression and identity such as race, class, and gender. It was developed in 2005 by the Disability Justice Collective, a group including Patty Berne, Mia Mingus, Stacy Milbern, Leroy F. Moore, and Eli Clare. There are 10 Principles of Disability Justice to follow when using this construct in the work of change.[3] It is unfortunate that over the past few years it has been co-opted to conform to the disability rights movement's white supremacist construct.

Equity is creating systems that are fair and impartial. The use of the word *equity* has taken on some interesting concepts. In public administration there is the theory of social equity, which means that equity is for all people. Many have taken on the use of *racial equity*, which does not exist because equity is creating fair and impartial institutions. It does not encompass the multi-marginalizations created by racism and white supremacy. No one uses the terms *LGBTQIA+ equity* or *refugee equity*; these are misnomers, as is *racial equity*, and should not be used in the work of ending oppression.

Erasure—the act of erasing—is to eliminate or scoop out completely. This is done over and over again in multiple areas of the disability rights movement but especially in the historical telling of the movement, which is dominated by white disabled advocates and centers white disabled experiences. There are few to no books, documentaries, or events that center BIPOC disabled activists who were most definitely leaders and part of this work. Many of the white disabled leaders also never discuss or name these BIPOC disabled activists in their many interviews, retellings, or books about the work.

Lived experience is a term used by activists to refer to people who have actually experienced any or all marginalizations, such as being unhoused, incarcerated, uneducated, etc. It is used to identify those who know the problems and are closest to the solution. Directly impacted are people who are related to those with lived experience. A child with an incarcerated parent or parents is living a life impacted by this marginalization.

Misogynoir is a term used to refer to the dislike of, contempt for, or ingrained prejudice against Black women. The term was coined by Black feminist author Moya Bailey in 2010 in an article discussing misogyny toward Black women in hip-hop music. It is a word blending *misogyny* and *noir*, which means Black in French. The foundation of the term comes from Intersectionality. Bailey created the term to describe misogyny directed toward Black transgender and cisgender women. It is rampant in the disability rights movement, for which they have been called out on many times to no avail.

Multi-marginalized is a term coined by me in 2014. It came out of the continuous frustrating conversations with white disability rights advocates, who condescendingly denied BIPOC disabled people the right to fight for their other marginalizations. It was used to explain intersectionality in the lives of BIPOC disabled people. Their disability is a portion of their disenfranchisement, and the fight to end systems of oppression must be included in their multiple marginalizations. BIPOC disabled people, in addition to their disability, are also of different faiths and are refugees, immigrants, LGBTQIA+, formerly incarcerated, and other. This is not accepted by many white disabled advocates. *Multi* is short for multiple, not multiply—we are not multiplying these marginalizations.

New world order is an explicit demand and needed reconfiguration of power as an outcome of the work of Black liberation. The result is having a majority if not all of the organizations doing this work being led by Black people. The order of the world today is that white people are the center of creating systems changes even when they entail the dismantling of their own white supremacy. This is rampant in the nonprofit industrial complex. The industry is dominated by leaders of organizations with mission and vision statements touting their work that centers the ending of racism through racial justice and creating equity. Yet the majority of the leaders are white people and in particular white women with no lived experience, no connections, to the communities living in trauma and a long history of actually being part of the problem. This is the disability rights movement, one that is long overdue for an overhaul and a reconfiguration of leadership.

Nonprofit industrial complex is a term that is a play on words from the term *prison industrial complex*. It is used to describe the attitude and work environment of many nonprofit organizations over the years that has created a replica of the same harmful and traumatic atmosphere for BIPOC and multi-marginalized people from the corporate world. It is believed that working for nonprofit organizations would provide safer and more just workspaces, but this has been disproven by many employees, specifically disenfranchised employees, of these organizations and especially in disability rights nonprofit entities.

Paternalism in disability is the assumption that disabled people need to be healed, cared for, supported, or managed for their own good without care for their individual will or ability to do so on their own. It is a form of advocacy that dominates the disability rights movement, especially in DC.

Pro-Black is a term used by Black liberation activists doing the work of ending systems of subjugation that refers to centering Black people in the work. It is not enough to be anti-racist. There is an imperative need to intentionally center Black people and Black disabled people in particular in the work of dismantling the barriers of oppression. The Black community must lead this work, creating a new world order, one where white people no longer are in leadership positions. It is the denial of white advocates and policymakers of this fact that continues the cycle of oppression especially in the disability rights movement.

Solidarity encompasses love in that it creates the shared awareness, values, concepts, interests, and standards needed to create economic, political, religious, and social change. In the work of collective liberation, it is a necessity for the creation of systems change. There is little to no solidarity within or outside the disability rights movement; this has been proven many times, like in the passage of the ABLE Act in 2014.

Trauma is the lasting emotional response that often results from living through a/multiple/continuous distressing events. There are three types of trauma: (1) acute, from a one-time event; (2) chronic, which is repeated and prolonged; and (3) complex, which is varied and multiple, often invasive and/or interpersonal. Many Black disabled activists have described their time working in the disability rights movement as traumatic from all categories.

Vulnerable is an adjective that means being susceptive to physical or emotional attack or harm. It is a word that does not explain why people are living the lives they live. There is no statutory definition of the word *vulnerable*. We are all susceptible to physical or emotional attack or harm. What has happened to BIPOC and all multi-marginalized people was purposefully done with malice; this is something we as a country are almost ready to admit. Most use the term *vulnerable* to make themselves feel better. They are not comfortable using the terms for what happened—*disenfranchised, marginalized.* These are verbs that explain the actions—the racism, the malice, the purposeful actions. People who are living the lives they live in poverty, unhoused, uneducated, and all other marginalizations, are doing so because of racist and ableist systems created specifically to disenfranchise and marginalize them. White people did this—a truth we as a country continue to run away from especially in language that describes that history.

White fragility is a term that describes the discomfort and defensiveness on the part of a white person when confronted with information about racial inequality and injustice. It was coined in 2011 by author and scholar Robin DiAngelo.

Whitewashing is the dictionary definition of the act of glossing over or covering up vices. But over the years many BIPOC activists have used the term to define how the white community takes social justice issues and removes and denies any connection to the white supremacist, patriarchal, and racist foundation of this country. In disability rights this is done in almost all policy issue areas. One is education policy for disabled students. There is little to no policy or advocacy work done on school climate and discipline, which includes but is not limited to the removal of law enforcement in schools and the dismantling of corporal punishment.

CHAPTER I

BUILDING AN ACTIVIST

All my life, I have questioned authority, wherever I found it. When I was two years old, I would pull my toys out in my mom's just-cleaned living room. "What are you doing?" she would say to me. "I just cleaned this house! You're messing up my living room!" To which I would reply, "This is my house too, Mommy!" I even had a fourth-grade teacher, a nun, write on my report card something like, "Dara has no fear! This could be a problem for her in the future. We may want to work on extinguishing this type of behavior."

This was in the '70s, long before the "school to prison pipeline" was identified or acknowledged. But my mother, an educator herself, read the code in that message on her Black child's report card. She took matters in her own hands, not only going into that school and assuring the staff that my safety would always be of the upmost importance for them. She also proceeded to inform them, as only a Black mother could, "You worry about educating her! I will worry about socializing her."

So when people ask me, "Have you always been like this?" I have to say, "Yes! Isn't everyone like this? Doesn't everyone call out and push back on authority?" In the home I grew up in, pushing back against authority was the norm, and my parents never once told me to calm down. They always had my back. My mom told me early on, "As long as you tell us the truth, we will always protect you."

Much later on, this is the spirit of pushing back on authority that I took into the policy world in Washington, DC. In my work as a policy person, I was having a conversation with a cohort about the unconscionable way an executive director of a new disability rights organization in "the community" conducted themself. This person named their organization a known racist analogy, proceeded to be forward and overt about how they believed BIPOC people were inferior, and constantly exhibited discriminatory thoughts and ideas. Some in the community would say they are "not *that* racist," as if there is a measurement of racism, while many BIPOC disabled people and I thought they were being covertly racist. I was not having it, and I let that person know that they were disrespectful, racist, and not welcomed in this community. But I stood with only a few and I was wondering why more would not stand up to this person and be the genuine civil rights advocates they claimed to be.

This person calmly said to me, "Dara, you do know that you are a unique person, right? That your lack of fear actually causes some in this community to be fearful of you!" Now, look, I do not think that I am unique; nor do I think that I am the only person doing this work who lacks fear. So many activists live and breathe the opportunity to create transformative change through collective liberation, therefore putting the lives of their loved ones and themselves in jeopardy. They are identified by law enforcement as terrorists for organizing communities to fight for themselves to create a better world. So I don't consider myself uniquely brave. I am one of many people fighting the good fight.

And I have learned from those who have been on the courageous path before me. I have spent most of my life reading and talking to my elders to learn about our history. It is my favorite thing to do when in the space of seasoned Black folk, to sit at their feet and hear the stories of my people. I have also been witness to many years of courageous and fearless activism, as well as my community just trying to survive every damn day no matter where we live.

———

In the election season of 2016, the racial tensions felt in the disability rights community came to a head, as it did for most of this country. This caused many in the community to rise up and say, "We have had enough." In that anger a group of us decided that no more will this community ignore overt and covert racism, which is used often in the national disability rights movement.

Through the National Disability Leadership Alliance (NDLA), a national disability rights coalition, we wrote a statement that was issued in October 2016. Neither that statement nor the group of people who worked on this has ever been taken seriously. None of the recommendations provided in the statement were earnestly worked on by the members or leaders of NDLA to create change. Instead, the majority continues to block any progress, while others in the community lack the courage to take action and create change. The statement we drafted is no longer posted on the NDLA website and has been erased from history.

Here is a part of the statement:

> Disabled people of color have been at the forefront of our movement from the beginning. Unfortunately, there has been a long and problematic trend in the disability community of the erasure and devaluing of the contributions of disabled people of color (POC). Lately, leadership in the

Disability Community has spoken more about race and Intersectionality than we ever have, but that in itself illustrates one aspect of the problem. As a community, it is necessary for us to acknowledge this history of erasure within our movement, actively work to promote Intersectionality, and elevate the voices of disabled people of color.

This erasure is just one of many examples of how working in this community has debilitated my psyche and essence as an educated Black woman. I am certain that I suffer from being a victim of overt and covert racism on a continuous basis. The definition of a victim is a person who suffers from a destructive or injurious action. Month after month, for ten years, I had to confront numerous barriers created to suppress my unapologetic voice that sought to tell the truth. In 2019 I took a new position at an organization not part of the larger disability rights (DR) community in DC and subsequently left being in those spaces. I have been called a troublemaker and told that I am disrespectful and of course confrontational. The majority in the disability rights movement has let it be known that my constant insistence that multi-marginalization and specifically race be part of all conversations is a nuisance. My actions in personal situations, on social media, and in emails on my personal account have been sent to the leadership of my organizations of employment and used against me as a threat to "keep me in my place."

I have had people contact my bosses and suggest that I be removed from multiple jobs. These are things that I have rarely heard happen to my white counterparts. But this is done to me because I am "the Black girl" and my truth makes many feel uncomfortable. All of this has been discussed openly on multiple occasions, as I am brazenly public about how I am treated by those who claim to be in this work to create a better world for all people.

Of course this is not a reflection of all the people in this community. But in general that was my experience in the disability rights movement. I have been honored and blessed to create change, work on creating laws that change people's lives. In the past twenty-two years I have assisted with getting over twenty-five bills passed in Congress and sent to five different presidents' desks, Clinton to Biden. I even got some bills passed and signed by #45. I have also met some amazing people who I know will be lifelong friends. But it is a mixed bag of emotions being a policy analyst and activist in this field. I teeter between feelings of elation for making a difference in this world and of anxiety about the possibility of losing my career because I am vocal about the injustices I observe on a daily basis. In *The Souls of Black Folk*, W. E. B. Du Bois discusses the fact that the Black body is an actual problem in the United States: *"To the real question, How does it feel to be a problem?"*[1] In disability rights they tout that there is nothing wrong with their bodies, yet my Black body in the room, asking questions, pushing back, calling out racism and all other issues, was a problem.

―――――

My close comrades in these struggles listen to my analysis of the disability rights community and often ask, "Do you think change is coming soon?" My reply is "Yes." I believe change in the way disability issues are worked is coming soon and has already begun, because others outside of this community are demanding it and working to create a new and inclusive movement.

When people ask, "How do you do work in that environment?" I tell them that faith is my guiding light. I know there is a beginning, a middle, and an end to all things—of this I am absolutely sure.

I also get asked, "How have you lasted so long?" I tell them that it's because I am hopeful, and I learned a great lesson from my parents, that when faced with adversity, never change who you are.

I believe that my life experiences prepared me for this work and exact moment. Let me tell you a little bit about where I came from. This description of who I am and how I function in my professional work is a part of the basis for this conversation about my involvement in the disability rights movement.

I was born in Spain, as my father was in the Air Force during the Vietnam War. I grew up in East Orange and Newark, New Jersey. I was the only child of two civil servants who did well for themselves and afforded me a very good life. Some of the things they exposed me to, besides an excellent education, were all kinds of lessons, which often put me in rooms where I was either the only child of color or, almost always, the only Black child in a room.

Although I was attending school and those programs during the day, I had to come home to East Orange, or many nights I went to my grandparents' home in Newark (which is where I really grew up and spent most of my life). It was the 1980s, and both cities were epicenters for the "War on Drugs," and, as Michelle Alexander's eloquent and insightful book explains, examples of what she titles and many of us believe is *The New Jim Crow*.

I had cousins who were victims of the harsh and hateful criminal legal system. I lived and played in neighborhoods where not only were there drug dealers but pimps and prostitutes and a rampant and active "organized crime" community. Those who have seen the HBO hit show *The Sopranos* will remember that Tony and the crew did their work in the city and went home to the suburbs and wealthy cities of New Jersey (like Upper Montclair). They did not, as they say, "shit where they ate."

My parents sent me to Upper Montclair, a city that is as exclusive as its name sounds, to attend an elite private parochial school, Lacordaire Academy, which has been voted the number-one private school in Essex County for years. I had ten students in my class in fourth grade, and by eighth-grade graduation there were twenty of us.

I took two buses and walked three blocks to and from the bus stop in the rain and snow to my school for many years. Meanwhile, my fellow students were dropped off in fancy cars whose names I couldn't pronounce then, with drivers and sometimes nannies or maids to ensure their safe delivery to and from school.

For most of my professional career I have been one of a few or the only Black people in the room, and many times the only Black person in a position of leadership. I am sure many in my community can relate. Looking back, my experience at Lacordaire Academy gave me the social skills not only to survive but to thrive in systems that are completely controlled by wealthy white people. It was not a great experience, by any means, but I am fortunate for the skills I learned.

My fellow classmates treated me better than my so-called Christian Catholic teachers and administrators, who were mostly nuns. It was definitely a place where I learned to hone my endurance skills without losing my pride in who I am and the beautiful heritage of my Blackness. I was one of the first Black students to attend the school from elementary and go all the way through the high school and actually graduate.

I clearly remember when I was in eighth grade preparing applications for high school and my parents sat me down to discuss my next steps in life. They were the ones who took no mess from anyone and especially when it came to their only child. One year my mom went to the principal of the school and asked if we could do a Dr. Martin Luther King Jr. Day celebration. This was during the fight to make this historic civil rights leader's birthday a national holiday. She was met with a little resistance, but once the other mothers joined in with support, due to their children's nudging, the school agreed to do this and so started a few years of this celebration.

But it was not always like that, and I had several run-ins with my instructors that were for the most part racially motivated. In seventh grade I had a teacher who refused to answer my questions. I would raise my hand and she would just ignore me. I was not doing well on a few social studies quizzes and my parents asked me what was going on in the class. It was not a shock when I told them about this teacher not answering my questions or having any desire to assist me.

My mom made an appointment to meet with this instructor to discuss this issue. But on the morning my mom took off from work (she was one of the only mothers who worked, if not the only one), this teacher decided not to come in for the meeting. After a few choice words with the principal from my mother, that was the end of this teacher ignoring me in class. But this only lasted a few weeks, as she just could not get her racist self up to teaching a Black child. My mother always set a good example, and I've never forgotten these early lessons in standing up to racism.

I became resilient, as many Black children do, because I did not want to do poorly in class, and I did not want my mom coming to fight my battles. So I would write down my questions on a piece of paper and slide it over to one of my classmates. They would raise their hand and ask my questions. My friends in school were more loving and Christian than those in charge of our education who were nuns and women of the church.

This is how I function. When someone puts up barriers that hinder my progress, I find a way around them, sometimes in ways like this, where my oppressor is none the wiser. Then there are other times where I just can't help but be a bulldozer and knock them down directly and intentionally.

After five long years like this, my father made it clear that I did not have to attend the Lacordaire Academy high school if I didn't want to. We were in the kitchen; he had moved out by then but was always welcomed in my home especially for meetings about me. He thought that after all the years of so many covert and overt racist issues in my education that I would jump at the opportunity to leave and attend a new school.

I looked at both him and my mother without any fear and said, "I am not going to any other school. I filled out the application and that's where I am going to attend. These people are not chasing me away. You taught me to face my enemies and to never change who I am. I'm doing both by going to that high school and I will graduate from there as well." My mom looked over at my dad and said, "That's your child!"

This was a family joke. I was always "his child" when this staunch activist came out of me. This is because my dad has never attended a protest in his life. It's my mom who was out in the streets fighting "The Man." She was a voting rights organizer and lied to my grandmother as she gathered multiple neighborhoods of people in Newark to get on buses to go to Selma in 1965. My father was the behind-the-scenes activist; security is his thing.

———

My mom was an active member of her local teachers' union in Newark. She attended Newark State, which is now Kean University, on a full scholarship. Her degree was in elementary education. She loved teaching and started in the kindergarten classroom. The teachers' union offices were located on South Orange Ave. in Newark and my mom spent many weekend mornings volunteering her time for the cause.

I would be up the street at the Greta Reilly dancing school taking tap, jazz, and acrobatics. Some days when I was done with my classes, my mom would pick me up, or I would walk down to the union office. There, I would help out the women, as that is all I remember seeing in those offices, with the work. The room would smell like ink from the carbon papers. Most of my tasks were part of the assembly line, sending out letters and flyers. They would type out a letter that was going either to the state or federal legislature or to the press. I had no idea what was in those letters, but it was my job to churn out copies on the printing machine.

Back then the letter would be typed out on a typewriter and then that sheet would be placed on top of a sheet of carbon that recreated the words on the paper. I would stand on a chair and take the handle that was attached to a large drum and turn it in circles that would churn out one copy for each rotation. We would let those dry and then fold them into three parts and stuff them into addressed envelopes. I would sit with little disk sponges that sat in water and rub the envelopes and stamps over them to get them wet, not too wet or they would not stick. At the end of the day, sometimes late into the evening, the women would help to load my mom's Volkswagen with the finished product. I would hop in and we would take the boxes over to the main Newark post office.

Those experiences watching my mother be an active member of a union machine planted a seed in me for collective work. Her allegiance to that organization was pivotal to her professional career. It is where she made a name for herself and created bonds that would last until her death. She created better working conditions and higher wages for her fellow teachers. It was also where she earned her impeccable reputation as an organizer and lover of her city and community.

———

The person who emerged from attending this predominantly wealthy white private school for nine years was a seasoned, determined young Black woman. I attended a Historical Black College or University (HBCU), Florida A&M University (FAMU), for my first two years of college but then returned to New Jersey to finish my undergraduate degree. I attended Rutgers University Newark campus, which has been ranked the number-one diverse campus in the country for many years.

At the time I attended we had over a hundred languages spoken on campus. But that was among the student population, not the faculty. Yet again I was in an institution, and my education was, principally controlled by white people.

It was also during the time when students were protesting and demanding that the university divest from South Africa as part of the larger movement to free Nelson Mandela and end apartheid. It was a struggle even in a system that was considered to be run by "progressive and leftist" administrators. This fight was my first introduction to the indomitable Sister Souljah, who had graduated but still led this movement down at the main Rutgers campus in New Brunswick, while others fought this on the other multiple campuses around the state. It was a time in my life when I learned about policy in the classroom and activism in the streets. These are great skills for my current work in social justice. But before all of that, I would go through different careers and adversities.

———

My journey in the professional world has been very much like my experiences in my formal education years, where I thrived in places of adversity. I stumbled into a professional field during my final year of college. In the early 1990s, healthcare management was up and coming as innovative technology created new systems as well as positions in that field. My first position in the field was working as a receptionist on the night shift at one of the first MRI facilities in the country. After graduation I moved quickly into the main offices and then encountered what would be my first of many layoffs.

I recall going to my mom and crying my eyes out because I felt like a failure. Success was drilled into me so much and this setback shook me to my core. The love and support of my amazing mother was never-ending, and she yet again stepped to the plate during this difficult season in my life. By this time in our journey my mom had returned to her Christian roots and was attending church regularly. That spiritual influence on her life enlightened her keen abilities to bring strength not only to her own life but also to her only child's. She was unyielding about me having good physical and mental health all of my life. In her living room she let me cry until the tears slowed down. Then she took me in her arms and said, "You are a child of God and you will be OK!"

She proceeded to discuss our belief in faith and what that actually means to me by reciting the scripture of Hebrews 11:1: *"Now faith is the substance hoped for, the evidence of things not seen."* Once the sermon was over my mother talked about the practical things.

She reminded me that I had been working most of my life, even in college, and that I could and should take advantage of my unemployment benefits. My mom proceeded to tell me to enjoy some time off to regroup and re-center myself. She instructed me to think about what was next in my future. Finally, she said with the most honest conviction, "You lost a job, not your life! You are blessed to have a large family and you have surrounded yourself with loads of friends who care for and love you dearly! And that, my darling, is more important than any job, position, or career and don't you ever forget that, young lady!"

That was one of the most important lessons I learned about my professional life. It is something that I carry with me to this day and keep at the center of my work ethic. It is part of the strength that I use each and every day I am on the front lines of social activism. It is a piece of the armor that I used to protect myself daily in disability rights work.

––––

My mom was right, as I took that time off to decide what it was I wanted to do with my career. At that time I wanted to be a healthcare executive, and I worked to move into that field. About six months after this layoff, I landed a position doing just that in a small startup medical company. I was on the finance team and worked as an account manager.

The organization I worked for was located in Jersey City, New Jersey, and the staff was full of diversity. That would be the support staff. The executive staff, though, was completely white and male.

I was at the company for a total of four years and received multiple promotions—all of which increased my workload considerably. While my time at this company started off well, it did not end that way. I saw them fire good people and treat them with disrespect.

In December of 2000, I decided to leave that company and handed in my two-weeks' notice. I had no job and no prospects of a new position. I was contemplating going back to school to obtain my master's degree. The shock on my white male VP's face said it all. When you resign like this, organizations used to inquire about where you are going and if they can counter-offer what is luring you away from them. The VP did this and when my reply was "No, because I have no position. I am just leaving!" he was flabbergasted.

There was other drama that I had to deal with upon my departure. The president of this organization was a man who tried to intimidate me and make me feel as if I would never make it out in the "real world." His words were unkind and his actions were duplicitous. The strength I felt my final day as I walked into his office and "let him have it" is something that has carried me into my advocacy work.

I turned thirty-one that year, and I was done with being disrespected by so many people and white people in particular. As I left his office, I made a promise to myself: *Those days are over. Never again will I hold my tongue when in the presence of oppression at work.* This is an imperative skill set to possess for the work I do each day in fighting for civil, human, and environmental rights. I draw on that energy from those days each time I use my voice. It is that spirit of "I am Black woman, hear me roar."

I also made good on my promise a few years later: I returned to Rutgers University to obtain my master's in public administration. In the summer of 2003 I won a competitive paid internship with a wonderful organization. This internship was my first experience doing policy for a large organization. I fell in love with policy work immediately and knew that this is what I wanted to do with my life.

My first day in the office was interesting. This was the first time a person of color had won this internship. I started on a day when most of the office was out at a meeting, and I was there to fill out paperwork and get set up in my office. It was a lovely office in a beautiful space. The executive assistant was a middle-aged white woman who, without any normal introductory conversation, immediately let me know that she had the opportunity to go to college but that life had taken her in another direction. This is code for *"Black girl, don't think you are better than me because you are here as part of this impressive program for collegiate and graduate students."*

It was code that I emphatically decoded and made a note for myself for the future. This is how I start analyzing new white people that I encounter in the workplace. What I have learned is that those white people who start off with this superiority complex never waiver from their foundation. Relationships are like building a home. You have a foundation and, in my Black woman experience, if you start off with this negative, covert cynicism and sinister relationship with a white person at work, it remains at the forefront of everything you do with that person, the entire time of employment.

While I worked to obtain my education at Rutgers, I was also part of a number of student groups that were actively working on campaigns to change things at the university. One group protested once a week for a fair wage for all Rutgers employees. This group was started by the teachers' assistants, who embraced the right of the janitorial and other staffs to bring home decent wages and have benefits.

I was raised by two union members—my mom, an educator, and my dad in law enforcement. There were many days that I spent with my mom working on voting and education rights. I took those skills that I learned being by her side and would have voter registration and education drives on campus all the time. I was actively involved in voting rights, but I have never been involved in politics. I have never worked or volunteered for a political campaign. That just did not get my juices flowing.

What did get me excited was activism, and what I instantly loved and knew to my core was my calling: public policy. It was in graduate school that I learned what public policy actually was and that it could be a profession.

These experiences in my youth and early professional career in healthcare are significant, for they are my foundation for my work ethic. They are what shaped me. Being in the corporate world provided me with a keen ability to sniff out covert racism and connect those dots to the racist people behind those actions. My prior career experiences also provided me a hard shell of protection that guided me in learning how to take no bullshit from anyone at any time. But fighting does not protect you from trauma; in fact, it is a significant part of the ordeal.

All my life, through college, through my first, second, and now third professional careers, I was often the only Black person in the room. In meetings about disability issues, this pattern repeated, as I was often the only person of color doing policy work, attending meetings, and advocating for disability rights in DC.

Because I am an educated Black woman who somehow got into the room and speaks well not only about disability rights issues but also about race, equity, and other multi-marginalized communities' issues, I was expected to be the "good Black girl" in the room. I was to act accordingly and never create spaces of discomfort that generate anxiety or fury by mentioning race, sexual orientation, or any other multi-marginalized groups' concerns.

———

Working in this movement, I have felt a mixed bag of emotions. I have feelings that have been with me all of my life in these situations. Being "the only one" usually means that I have to be the voice and the example of an entire community. Because of the lack of representation of other disenfranchised groups as policy staff in the disability rights movement, sometimes I had to do this for other oppressed communities.

For example, I am not Black Latinx and I don't identify as LGBTQIA+, as I do not come from those places of experience for these communities. Yet I was expected to communicate their issues when the opportunity arose. Because if I did not, then those communities' experiences and concerns would not be discussed or included in any strategy for change. The sad truth is that there is no solidarity. In fact, there is no mutual aid or cooperation for the "evolution of this social institution" in the disability rights movement.

This is the erasure of those with lived experience. Yet in the disability rights community, they live by a mantra "Nothing about us without us!" Even the history behind where and how this term made its way into the disability rights movement erases the two South African disability activists who started using it first.

I invoke this mantra used by a white-centered movement, because the irony is that when they say "us," they are not including BIPOC disabled people. This is made clear by the work of the community. When those of the multi-marginalized communities demand to be part of "us," their call for solidarity is ignored by the white disability rights majority.

Many have tried to address these problems but to no avail. There are multiple reasons they fail at these attempts "to smooth" things over when it comes to addressing the problems in this community. I'll discuss this in detail later in the book, but it's worth reviewing here.

These reasons are motives that do not originate from true solidarity. White disability rights advocates come from a position of white privilege and lack the recognition that there are actually problems of racial marginalization. As a result, they push back on those who want change. They have a profound inability to intentionally address those who have caused harm (racial and other types) in the community and a lack of desire to engage in any type of healing to start resolving these issues.

The disability rights community addresses resolving these racial concerns with the need for reward, not for creating a better society. What do I mean? They will write grants and tell funders that they are engaging in anti-racism work, but they have only engaged in writing that grant with no genuine or intentional change within their organizations. Many call this "doing the dance for the finance," and this is prevalent within the nonprofit industrial complex. There is a grave lack of intentional community and relationship building within the disability rights movement, and until this is addressed not much will change. In disability justice, collective liberation is essential to the work.

I worked in disability rights for ten arduous years. I was introduced to the field by chance, and my first position was to implement a grant set to increase the number of people of color involved in the movement. There remains a lack of BIPOC and other multi-marginalized communities working in public policy for the largest disability rights coalition, Consortium for Citizens with Disabilities, now known as Consortium for Constituents with Disabilities (CCD), with over one hundred organizations in DC that work on disability issues.

When I explain that I was the only POC and Black person in these coalition meetings in my speeches around the country and even in DC, there is an audible gasp of disbelief. I always pause and let what I said sink in. This has not changed much, even in 2022 with the racial justice reckoning of the summer of 2020 and the engagement that many organizations have taken on in diversity, equity, and inclusion (DEI). Yet, in DC disability rights policy positions there has been little change. The staffs remain white.

On the other end of this, there are few disabled people working for civil, human, environmental rights, and faith-based groups in DC, as there is a scarcity in hiring and putting people with disabilities in public policy positions or positions of leadership in those organizations.

I come from a space of awareness and authentic solidarity. I have invested my time and energy in learning about other communities' concerns so that I can embrace their needs and desires in my public policy work. It would be nice to see this type of outreach reciprocated in our nation's capital, where so many of us are fighting for justice for all people and a number of others are not.

CHAPTER 2

CREATING A POLICY MAKER

My entry into the disability rights community in DC was done through the most common way jobs are obtained in that place. I came to the nation's capital in November 2007 with no job and no prospects. Yes, I was unemployed, but I had an education, a village of mentors, talent, and hope. I did some contract work for the first two years. I remained active in my professional organizations and went to countless coffees, cocktail hours, and lunches and met more people who all said, "Keep in touch and let's see what we can do for you!"

But there are two things worth knowing when you hear those words in DC. First, never forget or lose touch with the person who said them to you. You never know where they may end up working in DC. Several of the people who said them to me worked in the Obama administration or currently work in positions of leadership for large organizations or are nationally known activists changing people's lives today. Second, don't rely on those words alone. As in any career, it's the "hustler" who gets the prize, and as they say, "Don't hate the hustler; hate the game." DC is unquestionably a place made by and for the masters of the game.

After two years of contract work, my largest job, with the National Legal Aid and Defender Association (NLADA), came to an end, and I had no idea what was next. I got a call from one of those people I had coffee with about six months prior, and that person put me in touch with the executive director of an organization who, she said, "needed someone with your talent." I met with that ED and within three days I had a position as advocacy manager at TASH, a disability rights organization, and so began my career with the disability rights movement. That was October 2009.

The reason I came to the nation's capital with no job in 2007 was because I had been "let go" from my previous position as a public policy staffer for a child advocate organization in New Jersey. I graduated with my master's degree in May 2004, and after my wonderful policy internship I knew what I wanted as my next career. In August 2005 I started in a small nonprofit in New Jersey. The office was, of course, full of white women in senior-level leadership and made up the entire policy team. This was a fact even though the organization's offices are located in the heart of downtown Newark, New Jersey, a city with a majority-Black population, across from the Rutgers campus.

People have a serious problem dealing with authenticity coming from an educated, strong, boisterous Black woman. I am not alone in this struggle, as many of my Sistahs have written about being in these situations. They discuss navigating the racist labor force in this country, which does not exclude the nonprofit industrial complex, where social justice work is principally done.

I was told, "You're just not a good fit." This was their reality. So I guess I was not a good fit, and sometimes God pushes you out the door to the next best thing in your life, because I am not so sure had this firing not happened to me that I would have gone to DC with no job opportunities. Thank goodness I did.

This new position as advocacy manager in the disability rights movement provided me the opportunity to meet and work with a number of executive directors of disability rights organizations. Prior to taking this position, I was aware of these groups through reputation and name recognition only, like many know The Arc. This was because these organizations do not actively participate in movement coalitions. I was the program director at TASH working on a project set to increase diversity and cultural competency at multiple levels within their organizations.

It was not the policy work I had my heart set on, but I was given the chance to update my title. The ED of the organization gave me an opportunity to do a little policy work in addition to the program work. It was in this new position that I was introduced to a broader section of the disability rights community in DC.

I came to the disability rights community at a time when it was insulated, because mainstream civil rights groups, in their words, "ignored them and their issues." They only worked with each other and on their issues of concern. There were "the players" and "the watchers," as there are with all group dynamics.

Education policy was the area I was given to work on for my organization. This work would be done with Consortium for Citizens with Disabilities (CCD), and my ED sent me over to the Education Task Force meetings. At the time the room was full, with about twenty people attending from different organizations. This is a common practice in DC coalition work. There is a vast amount of work to be done, and many organizations break it up among their fellow partners.

I was used to working in coalitions, not only in DC but back in NJ, where I was a child advocate. I was also an active member of my AME church, where I worked on several committees, and in a number of civic organizations, like my sorority (Delta Sigma Theta Sorority, Inc.) and the League of Women Voters, where I was also a chair of many committees. I also worked on national committees through these same groups, as well as through my professional organizations. So this collaborative work was not new to me.

At this time, I had been in DC for two years working in public policy for most of that time. In my consulting work I had the opportunity to serve on several coalitions around the city. Some of those coalitions worked on criminal and juvenile justice, employment, housing, voting rights, and a few other issue areas.

I was well aware of the dominant white progressive leadership in DC, because of my contract work done years prior. It is astonishing that even in those policy circles that discuss issues such as education, housing, criminal and juvenile justice, transportation, and other issues that affect a majority of communities of color or those who are multi-marginalized, the dominant people sitting at the tables were, and remain today, white people. Usually, white people are not only attending but leading those groups, and they are usually people with no lived experience. This has been a long-standing problem in many progressive movements.

The feminist movement is one example. This is so eloquently discussed in the amazing book *How We Get Free: Black Feminism and the Combahee River Collective* by Kee-anga-Yamahtta Taylor. Taylor engages with four amazing Black feminists (Barbara Smith, Beverly Smith, Demita Frazier, and Alicia Garza) to address this phenomenon and why it persists even in these times. Many Black feminists broke away from the mainstream feminist groups and created their own agenda and tables. This type of dichotomy continues as many create independent paths for dismantling racism and advancing the lives of Black and Brown people today.

One example that continues to annoy and insult many is the annual celebration of the passage of the Nineteenth Amendment. There are vast numbers of in-person and viral celebrations every year for this law that gave "Women the Right to Vote." What is ignored and even erased from this celebration is the fact that not all women got the right vote in the Nineteenth Amendment. Women of color, Native American, and disabled women were left out, and yet this never comes up in conversations held for this celebration. I have discussed this with a number of white feminists in DC and they do the same thing they always do when confronted with race issues by saying things like, "Oh why do we have to bring up race in this" or "Yes this is true but . . ." My reply to them is "When you do this, you erase my and many other disenfranchised groups' history. It is disrespectful and should be addressed by updating your titles to 'white women got the right to vote.'" There's nothing wrong with this, as it is a fact.

While the conversation about critical race theory centers around conservative white people denouncing our history, we must not ignore the fact that progressives, and in particular progressive white women, have been doing this for years. It is evident in the description of history that white feminists select what to discuss and display. There is a fourteen-foot-tall monument that unveiled in August 2020 in Central Park where Sojourner Truth is depicted as sitting at a table in strategic conversation with the known racist Susan B. Anthony.

This was done even though many Black women protested and continue to let all know that this sculpture is an insult to Black feminist history. But it is an open secret that any pushback by Black activists makes many white feminists uncomfortable, and that is never allowed. But the rest of us can be uncomfortable participating in celebrations and viewing art that is insulting and has nothing to do with our heritage and ancestors.

———

When I started working in civil rights policy in DC, even at those task force meetings where I was sitting and working at the table, there were some if not many BIPOC policymakers. This was not the case in the disability rights coalition. When I walked into the room for those education task force meetings, I was the only person of color. There were no people of other diverse backgrounds such as Asian, Latinx, Native American, or any other race.

At first I thought maybe some people were out on vacation and that I would see some people of color at the next meeting. But then the next meeting came and yet again I was the only person of color in the room.

Consortium for Citizens with Disabilities is like other policy coalitions that have multiple task forces and hold monthly meetings of all the leaders of these groups. This monthly meeting is open to all members of the coalition, even if you are not a co-chair of a task force. I decided to go to the monthly leaders' meeting and hopefully encounter some other BIPOC who work on issue areas like housing, employment, ADA, civil rights, and financial security. But I sat in that room and there was no other person of color who attended that meeting. Those in the room did not find anything wrong with this scenario. In fact, they were insulted when I asked, "Where are the Black policymakers?" Their response? "Why do you have to bring up race at every meeting we hold?" These things remain in play today.

I thought maybe the people of color were not chairs of the committees. That explained it, right? So I went back to my office and asked my ED if she knew of any people of color in the disability rights coalition who worked on public policy. She looked at me as if I had two heads and said, "Yes, yes, of course there are." It took her about ten minutes to come up with two names and their organizations.

I wrote their names down, found their contact information, and sent both of them introduction emails. They were, of course, close friends of each other and were shocked that a Black woman had been hired by my organization to work on policy. One of them worked around the corner from my office and invited me to an education group meeting they ran that was different from CCD. This happens a lot in DC. There are specific issues or campaigns that organizations want to work on or lead, so they will create a smaller working group either due to frustration with the larger group or the need to include others who are not members of the larger coalitions. It is all quite territorial in DC, even in social equity and social justice work.

Later that week I headed around the corner to the office for the meeting that was a small and intimate gathering of a few education policy people. The meeting was led by the person I talked to, and for me that was not only exciting but comforting. Here was a Black woman leading a meeting on an education policy issue in DC, which is a rarity. I stayed behind as the others left the meeting. She walked me around the office of this disability rights organization and introduced me to the staff. The entire policy and legal staff were white and almost all were over the age of fifty-five. The people of color, all Black, were the support staff, again a common occurrence I had seen in the disability rights organizations and greater civil rights organizations in DC.

She and I spoke for over an hour. First she praised me "for getting into disability policy work" and then asked, "How did this happen?" I was shocked by her surprise. I told her the story of my networking and how that had led me to my organization. The conversation was interesting, and she had deep insight into the community. She had been working in disability rights for a number of years. The most important things that I took from our fellowship were her deep concern for my mental well-being and her insistence that I keep that at the forefront of working in this community. That was the beginning of a long relationship of self-care that lasts to this day.

The other person of color I spoke to was a Latino man who worked on education and a few other issue areas. They both told me that they did not show up for those coalition meetings in person. They phoned in and preferred to work in that capacity. Now, I am a person who does not like to work over the phone and am a true believer in the value of face-to-face meetings, especially when working on such important issues.

But I slowly learned exactly why they chose to call-in for these meetings. It had nothing to do with their busy schedules or their ability to get to the sites of the meetings. Constantly sitting in rooms full of people who do not look like you and don't represent the communities you are working for has a seriously foul effect on your mentality. Unfortunately, this remains the case for me in the DC disability rights community. It's thirteen years later and even though I no longer work in disability rights, when I have to attend meetings with this community, I am usually the lone BIPOC in most rooms.

I was making a lot of friends in this new disability rights work at the same time that I was trying to figure out the politics of this new community. Those friends were instrumental in my decision to stay on, and some of them continue to be a fortress of strength and protection for me, when they can. My new colleagues and friends were mostly white women who had worked in this community for decades and they saw something rare in my work.

I have always been and forever will be unapologetic in my activism. My input brought a perspective to the work that was of course suppressed for years, as the voices of disenfranchised communities were and continue to be erased from this work. I also have worked with many communities in multiple ways, from grassroots organizing to congressional visits, and I knew how to use those talents to create new ways of doing public policy for disability rights.

I worked with other coalitions around the city, so I decided to take some of these disability issues, like dismantling restraint and seclusion, to the other civil rights coalitions outside of disability. The disability rights groups were talking to each other, and they were comfortable doing their work in these silos. This remains their modus operandi today as well. But this is not how I was trained to get issue work done, and I was craving to be around "my people."

I discussed this with my ED and obtained permission to get our organization to join a larger civil rights coalition called the Leadership Conference on Civil and Human Rights. Once we joined, I started going to the education work group meetings. I brought forth some of the information about restraint and seclusion to these new groups, and they were eager to assist. I not only felt like I had achieved some good movement on this issue, but I finally ended a day with some joy at being in a room with people who looked like me doing the same work. It was just one of the many tools that my colleague who was a person of color gave me to keep my mental well-being at the forefront of this work in disability rights.

————

In DC there are many coalitions that work on multiple issue areas in civil, human, and environmental rights. These groups have a number of task forces (TFs), committees, and working groups. For example, they usually have a Housing TF and a Reentry Working Group, and there are chairpersons for these groups. In most coalitions, those people represent their organization, and they are usually a person with some expertise in the subject area. The housing task force will be chaired by a person who works for a national housing rights organization, for instance.

These TFs and working groups meet monthly to discuss the issues at hand and gather on a more frequent basis when a "crisis" or threat to the community arises. This happened in early 2017 with the fight to save the Affordable Care Act. I want to lay this out for those who are not aware of how DC civil rights coalitions work and how all of this comes together for what is happening in the disability rights community.

This process of collaboration is no different from that found in many civic or religious groups, from which many of these coalitions have their foundation. As I discussed earlier, I grew up in an African Methodist Episcopal (AME) church that my grandmother attended, and this was how the social justice and community outreach in our church functioned. I am also a member of Delta Sigma Theta Sorority, and I grew up in a Delta house as my mom was also a member. This is exactly how all that amazing work gets done, through highly effective committees full of strong and dedicated Black women. Attending those meetings provided me with clarity about who controlled the agenda and why they only worked on issues of importance to those at the table.

These coalition groups also hold an annual meeting that provides an opportunity to mix and mingle with others you may not know or see because they don't attend your TF meetings. Some of the other staff members in organizations also attend these annual functions. The annual meetings have fellowship and fun with a raffle and getting-to-know-you games. The meeting itself is a combination of annual report out for each TF as well as handling the organizations' leadership business. There are reports from the treasurer and secretary, annual addresses by the leaders (president, chair, etc.), elections for new officers, and presentations of appreciation for departing leaders.

In January 2010 I attended my first annual meeting of CCD. I had been with my organization for just a few short months, and I was interested in how this meeting would function. In the few months of working in this community, I learned that there was little to no representation of multi-marginalized communities, and I mistakenly thought that would be different at this annual meeting. The meeting was held at the Henry J. Kaiser Family Foundation DC building in the Barbara Jordan Conference Center, named after the amazing and powerful Black Democratic congresswoman from Texas.

I arrived early as usual and entered this newly built entity with awe and sincere reverence for one of my idols. I was also struck by how much life had changed. Just five months prior I was unemployed sitting in my empty living room with no job prospects and hysterically crying to the one person who loved me more than anybody (my mom) that my dream of doing policy in DC was over. Fast-forward and here I was in the middle of DC attending an annual meeting of a national disability rights coalition as the representative of my organization. The smile on my face was nothing compared to the joy in my heart. I had finally gotten my foot in the door of this policy world, and I was hopeful.

The Kaiser Family Foundation building sits in the heart of DC and is a few steps from the White House. It is a glass-encased building, and on the first floor is the media center. When one enters the building, the staff is welcoming and wonderful. They send you up the beautiful staircase to the second floor (there is an elevator for those who need one).

As I climbed the stairs and headed to the second floor, I saw to my left on the wall Barbara Jordan reigning over the room just like she did in life. It was one of the iconic pictures of her made into a beautiful sculpture on the wall. Of course there was an inscription below her portrait that gave her date of birth and death and a brief history of why this room and meeting space was named for this magnificent woman. I did not need to read because she was one of the people who influenced me to do the work I was embarking on and why I was in that space for the annual meeting. I am blessed for so many reasons but also because in my life I had the honor and privilege to not only meet but sit and talk with a number of my sheros, and Barbara Jordan was one of them.

The fact that CCD was holding its annual meeting in a room named after one of the most iconic Black figures in modern political history was not lost on me. But it was lost on those organizing the meeting. How do I know? I inquired and spoke with the new chair of the organization.

I went into the Barbara Jordan room, which is a sophisticated meeting center with all the bells and whistles: screens on multiple walls, comfortable seats placed in auditorium style facing the stage, beautiful lighting. There was a ramp positioned just to the right of the stage that I thought would be used for someone with a physical disability. In the middle of the room standing and preparing for the meeting was the upcoming new chair. I had met her at a few TF meetings, and we were friendly.

I walked over and we did hellos. I then asked her, "So are you planning to say a few words about the room we are meeting in?" She looked at me with that puzzled and exhausted look, and it was at that moment I knew she had no idea who Barbara Jordan was or that she should be honored in this way.

She replied, "Well no, should we?" I asked her to join me in the hallway and revealed to her the lovely sculpture and tribute to Representative Jordan. I saw a glimpse of her acknowledging that Jordan was important. Yet at no point did I see recognition of who this woman was in the political history of this country.

I sensed that she understood my desire to discuss Barbara Jordan. But she was hesitant about the need for something like this to be done at their professional annual meeting. It was yet another part of what was missing in this community by erasing the voices of those disenfranchised because of their race.

This is what cultural competency and diversity brought to the table for these organizations. Remember that I was at my organization implementing a grant just for this reason. I felt it was my duty to explain why this is important and hopefully open a door to start a conversation about why these voices are missing.

I proceeded to explain to her the importance of praising Barbara Jordan and her accomplishments at the beginning of the meeting, other than the fact that the Kaiser Foundation chose to give the conference center her name.

Communities of color give honor to those who came before us, and in many cases there are religious calls for grace prior to most assemblies and events. If you have ever been a part of a march, rally, direct action, protest, conference, or convocation for civil rights and social justice, there are moments when the leader brings a silence to the event and gives honor to the ancestors, the Indigenous people whose land we are on, or says a prayer to God, Allah, or Yahweh, and if needed to those who are being celebrated that day. It is a distinct method to ground and center our minds, hearts, and spirits for the purpose of the gathering.

To my surprise, after I provided this explanation, the woman who would be the next leader of this coalition said, "Well I don't really know about her and I would not feel comfortable discussing her. Would you mind doing this?" She asked the question because she is smart and knew she should not be the person to do this honoring. It was not only a clever move but one of great courage in this community. She was giving a microphone to a newcomer who would discuss a woman many in the room knew nothing about and would not understand why this was being done. The meeting convened with the standard opening of business gatherings, and with the addition to the agenda, things started for the 2010 CCD annual assembly.

Public speaking has never been an issue for me. I have been talking to large groups of people all of my life in my community and I am a loquacious person. I have not met a person I can't talk with yet. Highly important people or even the most hateful, disrespectful, and mean people are no match for my mouth or my tongue. I once had a dear colleague of mine describe my words as "a sword that comes in and cuts the heads off of people, stopping them in their tracks." I will admit that in this work there have been and will be times when that type of communication is not only necessary but completely appropriate to make my point.

This day in January 2010 was not one of those times. It was my opportunity to introduce this predominantly white community to a custom of many in the civil rights community. The time came and the woman introduced me. I walked up to the microphone and in my most eloquent and passionate voice provided a brief history of Barbara Jordan. She was a Democratic member of the House of Representatives from Texas, a civil and human rights icon, and accomplished so much for millions around the world in her lifetime. These were among the many reasons this amazing conference center was named after her. But the most significant justification was that she served on the Kaiser Foundation board. They recognized the heroic and loving work she did around the world to change the direction, for the better, of the HIV and AIDS epidemic.

She was a staunch civil rights activist who worked closely with the Congressional Black Caucus and her partner in policy and sorority sister, Rep. Shirley Chisholm (D-NY) to bring forth laws that changed the lives of millions. I also added that she was my sorority sister whom I had the opportunity to meet and sit with many times to discuss social action and justice outreach in our community. At that time I was unaware of the wonderful contributions Jordan had also given to the ADA; that knowledge would come later in my work.

It was amazing to be in that center named for her and to recount some of the great work she had done. I was filled with emotion because for the first time in a gathering of CCD, it felt like my community, Black people, had some value. Remember I had been attending TF meetings and sitting in rooms with all white people with no voices from other communities. I had met the two other people of color who purposefully chose to do this work from a peripheral position. It was the first time I was in front of the entire organization, and I was yet again hopeful.

When I finished my discussion of Barbara Jordan, which was only about five minutes long, there was a brief, tepid response. Barely anyone applauded and no one came up to me later to ask more about her or her work. They also did not thank me for bringing this to their attention and making this a part of the day's meeting. I was truly taken aback by the lack of response and interest. This was from a group of disability rights advocates who claimed to have a foundation in the civil rights movement. Yet they had no idea who those icons are or what that means. They of course always know and quote the usual suspect of Dr. Martin Luther King Jr., but beyond that there is no interest or respect for all the other soldiers in the movement.

I sat my emotional self down and trudged through the rest of the full-day meeting. Yet again I was attending an event in the disability rights community that was completely made up of white people. The staff members from Congress invited to speak about disability policy were all white. It is well known, and data has proven in two reports done by the Joint Center for Political and Economic Studies, one titled *Racial Diversity Among Top Staff in the US House of Representatives*, done in October 2022, and the other *Racial Diversity Among Senate Committee Top Staff*, done in July 2021. They both showed that Congress, like most institutions in this country, lacks staff diversity. Disability policy is mostly worked in the Education and the Workforce and the Energy and Commerce Committees in the House and in the Health, Education, Labor, and Pensions (HELP) and the Finance Committees in the Senate. Most of these committees at that time, in 2009 and 2010, had BIPOC staff members, and I worked with many of them on a regular basis. The rest of the disability rights community did not interact with those Black and Brown staff members and therefore had no relationship or connection to invite them to this meeting. This remains a practice in the work today.

Those receiving awards from the coalition that day were also all white, nondisabled people. That year they happened to be all women. It was interesting that even though there was a well-constructed ramp set up, not one person with a physical disability needed to use that ramp the entire day. No one with a visible disability went on that stage to participate in the meeting.

At our lunch break I went to the back of the room where many of my new friends were sitting huddled together in their wheelchairs, and I said to them, "Do you think anyone who needs to use that ramp will make it to the stage? I am not quite sure why they put that ramp there other than to be politically correct." We all had a good laugh. But then they got serious and told me about their experience of being left out of many of these events and positions of leadership. They were all too familiar with the bias and ableism of CCD.

At the end of the meeting, I went back over to that group and said "Don't feel bad. I did not see one person who looked like me today on that stage either. We've got work to do!" Many in that group remain my dear friends and have been helpful to me.

I made sure I spoke to the new chair of the coalition and expressed my appreciation for the opportunity to talk about Barbara Jordan. Then I proceeded to tell her a few of my observations. She was thoughtful and asked me to contact her so we could talk more about my concerns. It would be the beginning of eleven years of "Yes, Dara, I hear you, and we should talk about how to change this." I got the same reply from almost every person and specifically the leadership I interacted with in CCD. It remains a catchphrase for them today, with little to no changes and no prospects for any change in the foreseeable future. They are comfortable in their silos, and since there is no accountability for their work, the white supremacy and racism thrive.

———

What I learned that day about the disability rights community in DC was overwhelming. Not only were they exclusively white in their leadership and outreach work; they were completely nondisabled. It was an oxymoron to me because the mission and vision of CCD are to *create a community where people with disabilities are fully integrated into all aspects of life.* Yet in its own leadership and on many of its working task forces there was and is little to no representation of the very community they were supposed to protect and include. This would be the first day of my long and arduous road of trying to infuse the voices of and the policy issues of concern from those communities disenfranchised and multi-marginalized in this country.

That annual meeting made a lasting impression and influenced the work that I continue to do to this day. The work that I embarked upon was to implement Intersectionality. I wanted to include "in the streets activists" who were not only appreciated but also respected at the same level as all others in this movement. I am going to tell you what happened on that journey: the good, the bad, and the ugly.

———

I tried being hopeful about disability rights work, until I couldn't any longer. But the creation of the disability justice movement afforded me the opportunity to approach the work intersectionally.

It is necessary for this story to be told. The history, one of many imminent moments when multi-marginalized and disenfranchised communities demanded change, also must not go unnoticed or, worse yet, be forgotten. Many in the disability rights movement feel that they can just sweep this under the rug and move forward with creating a space that is open and ready for change.

But as many communities have learned, that is not how healing works. As in any relationship, in order to heal, the abuser must acknowledge the victims'/survivors' feelings and admit to the wrong that was done. This work on a political level usually entails what is called a truth and reparations period. These conversations and processes are done through government and non-state entities, as I'll discuss later.

It is essential to know history if you want to do social justice work. There must be a genuine acceptance and realization of the pain that racism, classism, homophobia, ableism, and all other institutional disenfranchisements in this country are the cause of the problems. This acceptance frames the entire purpose of all the civil and human rights work and specifically in the disability rights movement. Because if you do not know where you came from, how do you move forward and know where you want to go?

Many people both in and outside the disability rights community tell me they never knew this story about this movement. But it explains so much to them and what they observe. Those I am discussing this with in DC take a moment to ponder their interactions with the disability rights community and realize that, in fact, they only see white policy people at the tables.

That day in January 2010 at the CCD annual meeting, I
made a vow to Barbara Jordan and all my ancestors that I
would not forget this moment and that nothing would stop
me from being a changemaker. It is just a part of what drives
me every day to continue to demand respect, acknowledg-
ment, and that BIPOC communities are not just included in
the disability rights community but have leadership positions.

Many activists in social justice movement have no more
patience and are not waiting for white people to get "woke."
For many in the work of Black liberation, there is no longer
a need for white people to be comrades. It is time for us to
lead in creating systemic change from a place not only of
anti-racism but of being pro-Black.

Something in the world changed while I was making
strides in DC disability rights policy work. The invention of
the iPhone and social media blew up not only as a form of
communication but as a bridge that connected communities
around the world. The work of creating change through policy must be done "from the streets to the suites," and social
media did wonders for this approach.

In 2010, when I was at TASH, the ED hired a great communications person. He was young and excited with fabulous ideas for the work. One day he came to me and said,
"Can I see your phone?" I pulled out my flip phone and he
rolled his eyes. I was like "What? What's wrong?" He said,
"I want you to join Twitter and get information out to our
members when you are at meetings and on the Hill."

I was like "Twitter? What is that?" He brought me to
his computer and showed me what Twitter was and what
a tweet could do. He was brilliant. In 2010, he told me this
will be the next big thing in social justice movement, and he
wanted me to be an expert in how it worked. He set up a

Twitter page for our organization and gave me a few lessons but let me know that this was another on-the-job training kind of thing. Then he gave me the password for our Twitter page and sent me on my way. The ask was to tweet at least four times a day from any meetings I attended around DC.

The first day I set out for my meetings I was a bit skeptical. I thought nobody cared about where I was going or what I was doing in DC. Well, that was quickly debunked. There were people following our page and they were quite active. The first Hill event I went to was a hearing on the House side, and this was when tweeting first started so there were few to no hashtags and few members of Congress were on Twitter. But our comms person taught me to ask the staff when a hearing had a hashtag and this hearing actually did. I sat down and sent out a tweet letting our members know where I was and what the hearing was about for the day. In less than five minutes I had retweets and replies asking me, "Hey, is my congressman in the room? He's on that committee and he should be in the room!" I replied "Yes!" or "No!" If I said they were not in the room, the person let me know they were calling the office to ask why that member was not at that hearing discussing disability issues.

I was completely amazed by this. Here I was in a House hearing room in Washington, DC, and a person clear across the country was able to connect in real time and get information they could not get otherwise or from any other source. Hearings on disability issues are rarely if ever shown on C-SPAN or cable news, as they don't garner that type of media attention. This realization sent chills through me. This was a tangible outcome, working from the streets to the suites to create change. I had an immediate love for Twitter and its power of connecting people.

Even though I had that old flip phone, I set out to learn everything I could about Twitter and tweeting. I refused to get an iPhone because back then I would have had to give up my phone number to get a new phone, and that was not happening. I used that flip phone, and my comms person and I became experts at growing our Twitter following and activity on the platform. I was completely involved in Twitter. I used to tweet live at night watching some TV shows. It was a way for me to increase my skills and learn how this platform functioned. I was obsessed.

Soon I had my own Twitter handle and a pretty good following among disability advocates and BIPOC disabled people in particular. It was so wonderful to talk with people from around the country about their concerns, issues, and ideas for what advocacy should look like in DC. They all felt that the racist white disabled community dominated the narrative and work by centering their issues and ignoring BIPOC disabled people. It was disheartening for them to learn there were no BIPOC disabled leaders of organizations in DC. I can't tell you how many friends I have made through this platform even though I have not met many—they are my comrades in arms to this very day.

I really felt the power of Twitter one day when I was in a coffee shop and ordered a hot chocolate. They ask you your name and I said Dara. There were three people on line behind me that said, "Are you @NJDC07?," which is my Twitter handle. Now, I also know about security and that not everyone on social media has love for all, so I was hesitant with my answer. I slowly turned around and said, "Maybe, why?" "Wow! You are doing some amazing stuff! I didn't even know this stuff about disability policy!" My mouth was hung open and I was speechless—a rarity for me. They all said, "Yes! Keep up the great work! Oh and you should post more pictures!"

I ran into my office and told my comms person about this. His reply was, "You could post more pictures if you got rid of that old flip phone!" Really, that was his reply. At that moment I knew that this platform was yet another way for me to be successful in policy work outside the DC Beltway's predominantly white disability rights groups.

I used to go to strategy meetings about advocacy campaigns for upcoming Hill work and there would be the regular outreach tools—alerts, letter-writing campaigns, one-pagers sent to the Hill (Capitol Hill, the site of Congress)—but nothing on social media and definitely nothing done on Twitter. This was late 2010 and early 2011. Only a few Congress members were on Twitter. The White House was not on Twitter.

Once I moved over to the National Council on Independent Living (NCIL) in July 2011, I would go to meetings and push for Twitter to be a part of the campaigns. Many in the room laughed and even rolled their eyes at me when I would inquire if we had a hashtag. I would suggest that we send tweets to those committees and members who were on Twitter. I would do this not just in the disability rights community but also at housing, criminal justice, transportation, and other issue area meetings.

I tried to let these groups know that in a few years Twitter would be the way that the Hill communicated with the people and all members of Congress would have a Twitter handle. It was one of those things you could just feel. If you work with people and know what gets them excited, you could see that it was inevitable that each member of Congress would have a Twitter handle and a comms person who handled that page. By 2012, those same people were asking me where I learned about Twitter and how I got so good at being on the platform. I just smiled like I always do and said I had on-the-job training. Thank you, Jonathan (my comms person at TASH); you were fabulous to work with and you turned me on to the tool that would push me to a level of disability activism and recognition that I never thought I could attain.

———

Twitter not only connected me to active and passionate advocates. It pushed me into conversations that were happening around the country on the issues I worked on in DC. Those conversations gave me different perspectives, taught me about what was happening on the streets, provided me with reading materials and lists of experts in the field that no one in DC knew about or worked with, and opened my world to yet another group of people outside the DC Beltway.

Through my interactions on Twitter, I would let many out in the US know that I was the only Black person and person of color sitting at the tables for the disability rights conversations on policy here in DC. Many of the advocates elsewhere in the country were astonished by this fact. They would ask questions like, Why don't these groups in DC work on law enforcement and the killing of people with disabilities? Or, Why are these organizations not weighing in on the Voting Rights Act concerns that deal with race? I would reply that these were not issues of concern to them because those voices are not part of their membership, leadership, or staff. I was as usual my authentic self even on Twitter. I was honest about the white-centered policy agenda of the disability rights community in DC.

I had some serious "haters" from these DR groups I was discussing. They would either do things on Twitter with mean and hateful tweets telling me I was angry, wrong, and needed to be fired, or let me know by telling me to be quiet, you're causing trouble, and you need to learn your place in meetings. A number of them would call my bosses each week and tell them I should be fired. I even had people send emails to my bosses with the same messages. But I ignored them and had no concerns, because what I tweeted out to the world I said in those rooms on a constant basis. But I was just ignored by them in the rooms. That is part of the reason the whiteness of this community continues to thrive. It is an insular society only functioning within their own silos where accountability is ignored and removed.

But I was not ignored by those on social media, and they were there to support me in my frustration and anger. They also provided me with information about events, conversations, and conferences being held by BIPOC disability advocates who did care about these issues. This community was doing what I learned was the best way to get things done; they were going outside the disability rights community and creating their own community of activists. BIPOC disabled people were and continue to be changemakers and stay away completely from the disability rights community.

I am active with my own posts as well as following many others using these multiple platforms of outreach. My interactions on Twitter and Instagram have created comrades in the struggle to bring forth the information and work on multiple issue area advocacy campaigns that have changed lives. A large number of these activists remain great friends and some I have met in person. I respect them and consider them among the best policy minds in the country. They have been more than helpful through care and have created a wonderful space for me to do the work of Black liberation.

I have been on multiple speaking engagements and participated in multiple advisory committees and boards around the country because of these relationships, as they recommend me to others. They have also been instrumental in getting me in to congressional offices that would not be inclined to talk with me here in DC. It is not always easy to get into offices, but if you have constituents from that state, call in and ask the staffer to please speak to our DC policy person; they can open the door. My Twitter outreach provided me with opportunities to meet some advocates who came to the DC area. This was always a wonderful experience, and yes I use caution, meeting all in public places, forging great relationships, and working with many of them to this day on creating change.

———

When my stint at TASH came to an end, it was time for me to move on to a new and more career-oriented position. I also had some internal issues with my ED about how advocacy work should be done. Collaborative and inclusive work is where I thrive. I chose to take a huge pay cut and moved on to a policy position with my next organization.

It was a group that I respected because of its leadership and model of advocacy. This respect was there for the two years I worked with them and a few years after my departure from employment. But that respect is no more. Working for the National Council on Independent Living (NCIL), I experienced some serious issues with race, misogynoir, and many other forms of discrimination. In the end, I felt that I was treated as household garbage by the leadership.

But back to the large decrease in pay that I had to accept in order to work in my dream job of public policy. Yes, you read that correctly; I took a huge pay cut to make this move. As Denzel Washington said in one of his commencement speeches, "Don't just aspire to make a living. Aspire to make a difference!" Don't you just love words like this that come from multimillion-dollar wealthy people? But I got that a long time ago as I walked away from the corporate world one day with no job prospects, just my sanity intact and a heart full of hope to change the world. The lack of pay and the treatment of civil rights staff in DC is a subject for an entire book. There are several civil rights organizations that fight for living wages, paid leave time, and decent human rights in the workplace in their policy agenda and yet their own employees have had to create unions. The organizing and collective bargaining were not always met with enthusiastic or willing management. Remember these are civil and human rights organization leaders.

Another problem I soon encountered was the serious lack of corporate philanthropic investment in many grassroots organizations run by and for those directly impacted. Those within the nonprofit industrial complex have not improved outcomes in decades and have instead created a space that is simply exclusive and not led by people with lived experience.

Can you understand exclusive space in civil rights/social justice work that is not inclusive of those directly impacted? Neither can I, but believe me, it exists and remains alive and well today. Those of us who call it out are referred to as radical. Barriers are put in our pathways to success and we are expected to disappear or, worse, be quiet. As the amazing Black femme activist leader Charlene Carruthers says in her book *Unapologetic*, "Being radical is a choice, and it takes work."[1] I gladly wear the title of being a radical, for no oppressive system has been dismantled quietly or without unrest.

Here is a portion of the problem: "progressives" around the country feel like they are making a difference because they are fighting to create change. This may be true and I say "may" because this is debatable. Many BIPOC activists and policymakers argue with this thought process. They find much of the work being done by "progressive" white-led organizations to be that of creating even more harm and in no way working to transform the systems. The constant use of language by "progressives" is that of reimagining and reforming the systems, the very systems that are working as they were intended, with white supremacist, patriarchal, misogynistic, and racist foundations.

Take the war on poverty, which has been a movement led by white progressives for over fifty years now. The fight to end homelessness is another issue area led by white progressives for over fifty years. These organizations were in existence doing this work when the oppressive and horrific Bill Clinton and Joe Biden crime bill was passed in 1994. The BIPOC community is constantly told that the Democratic Party is the one that will "protect and serve" them, yet history has proven this claim to be wrong.

There are a number of things that many of these white-led "progressive" organizations lack in their work to create change. One is the commitment to the transformation of systems, which entails dismantling the power structure, one where they have the power. The transformation of systems removes them from having the power. Two is that for years they have lacked the desire to engage with genuine respect with those who are directly impacted. Those with lived experience are predominantly BIPOC, and purposefully having all-white staffs, leadership, and boards does not make this type of outreach possible. There is an absence of urgency and a serious lack of accountability for these white-led groups. It is for all of these and many more reasons that there must be a new world order. This entails white people removing themselves from the tables and in some cases the rooms.

A third problem is that "progressive" organizations refuse to embrace collective liberation as a pillar for creating a new world order. At the core of this is centering BIPOC communities, in particular BIPOC disabled. If you remove the barriers that harm and kill disabled BIPOC you will resolve the issues for all people.

And finally, "progressive" organizations lack the courage to be disruptors and say "No, this is wrong" to the power structure, in particular the Democratic Party. They want to enjoy their proximity to power more than they want to dismantle the issues and end all of this oppression. This holds true for the disability rights movement and is proven in their erasure of disabled BIPOC in almost every aspect of their policy work.

CHAPTER 3

KNOWLEDGE IS POWER

am not a person who follows astrology or numerology, but I respect that these beliefs exist in the world. My birthday is in the fifth month of the year and on the twelfth day. It was that day that I had my interview with NCIL. I had my second interview a month later, and my first day of work on a day that would change my life in DC was on 7/11/2011. It was also the first day of their annual conference. This was a perfect time to be introduced to the membership and leadership of the organization.

I attended and spoke on a panel at the national conference the year prior as part of my program on diversity and cultural competency project in my previous position. In that work I had the opportunity to meet a number of the board members and a few members of the diversity committee. NCIL is led by and for people with disabilities. It is membership driven and has a staff composed mostly of people with disabilities. This is in their charter and very much a part of the fabric of their work. It is what drew me to them, and every day I worked there I was immersed in my hope for change.

The annual conference used to be amazing with the panels and information they provide to membership and the conducting of business, as there are two board meetings that bookend the conference—one with the current board just prior to the start of the conference and one at the end with the newly elected board. During the conference there is an annual membership meeting where every dues-paying member has the opportunity to vote on the candidates for leadership. Dues for this organization are nominal, and there is a process for waiving them for those who may not be able to afford this amount.

The conference is always held in the nation's capital because at the core of the work is policy change. NCIL brings its entire membership to DC, where "the mountain" is, and with a well-organized policy strategy that has been worked on all year, they descend upon the Hill. NCIL used to run this way, but much has changed and not for the better.

My first conference as an employee in July 2011 was amazing. This was the first fully accessible conference, with American Sign Language (ASL) and captioning at every event, that I attended in my life. NCIL is still one of the few civil, disability, and human rights organizations that do this and do this for all of their meetings and events.

In these aspects this organization has been the outlier in the disability rights movement. They chose for years not to be a member of CCD, because it does not encompass the principles of inclusion and surely is not practicing them. Most of the members of CCD do not have organizations led by people with disabilities; their staffs are not full of employees with disabilities, and their programs are not accessible—webinars, conference calls, in-person meetings, and conferences. They do not have at the core of their work people with disabilities as leaders.

Even though NCIL encompasses most of these things in their work, they still have an issue with race, equity, and the inclusion of multi-marginalized communities. The difference is that just a few years prior to me joining the staff, they admitted this problem and made creating change a priority of their work. Hence, this is how they were part of the diversity project I was leading at TASH.

But NCIL remains steeped in oppression. There remains a large divide in the membership, with the majority, white disabled people, leading. They continue to deny they have problems and refuse to acknowledge that white supremacy, racism, and all other oppressions exist in disability rights. Unfortunately, NCIL is not much different from the other one hundred plus groups in CCD.

———

NCIL opted out of being a member of CCD for years. They had decided to leave because of the lack of any people with disabilities (at least with visible disabilities) in leadership positions, as well as the constant paternalistic outreach being done. But at the final board meeting for the 2011 conference, they decided to rejoin the coalition and to hold a large My Medicaid Matters Rally later in the year.

I was tasked with being the lead staffer on this campaign and I worked with three amazing advocates on getting this done by October. The rally would be held in Washington, DC, and would be a kick-off for a policy campaign to put at the forefront the importance of Medicaid for the disabled. Our team was made up of one board member, two other staff members from disability rights organizations, and me. I never met any of my partners but did get to know the board member at the conference. We started our work immediately upon returning to the office that Monday after all went home from the amazing conference.

My number-one task was to get sponsors for the event. It was my ability and experience with collaborative work that helped me get organizations to sponsor. There was only one criterion for joining the campaign: your organization had to recognize and accept that Medicaid expansion be done throughout the country. The Affordable Care Act (ACA) passed in March 2010, and this was imperative to the lives and liberty of people with disabilities.

The list of organizations to reach out to were of course the other disability rights groups in DC and around the country. I had been working with other civil rights groups in DC for about four years. In my NCIL position, I had the opportunity to go back and work on criminal and juvenile justice. I made inroads with the Leadership Conference and joined a few working groups. It was my goal to use those connections and relationships to persuade some of these organizations to sign on as sponsors for the My Medicaid Matters Rally.

At a very young age, I became aware of one of my best qualities. It is one that has catapulted me in my career and given me great success in changing lives. My maternal grandmother discovered and nurtured it in her home. I have a great rapport with people. Most of my connections to people are genuine and when they are good it is wonderful and when they are bad, well, they are horrors. I have a face that is inviting, and people tell me things even when I don't inquire about them. This amazing ability, along with my uncanny aptitude to remember faces and names, led to a nickname. I have been affectionately referred to as "the network queen."

I know there are probably many other nicknames out there for me. But I wear the title of "the network queen" with pleasure and a careful twist. Networking is equated with schmoozing; this I don't do. I am not a schmoozer; here is the twist—I am a connector. For this campaign I made fabulous connections and was able to garner a large number of civil and human rights organizations to be sponsors and actively participate at the rally.

This work entailed long hours and lots of conference calls with our core team and many others around the nation. I have been an organizer for many years, but this was intense. In the summer of 2011, I had just started in this position; was absorbing disability rights language, etiquette, and laws; and was trying to navigate this all-white public policy community. I ran into a few brick walls when talking with CCD members about joining the rally as sponsors. This was a new way of doing outreach that many did not engage in, and this set up a power shift in the community. Those with lived experience were leading this rally, something the DC Beltway crew had never experienced. Many of the CCD members did not participate in NCIL's annual conference. But with this work, those tides would be changing, or so we thought.

There was fear from others who did not know me and who did not want to participate in a "direct action." I was taken aback by this attitude and description of the My Medicaid Matters Rally. My response to these trepidations was, "Do you know what a direct action is? Because this is a rally, not a 'protest'! This is signaling to legislatures, policymakers, advocates, and communities around the country the imperative need for Medicaid and all its benefits for those with disabilities!" To coax many of them to get on board and be a part of the rally, I had to assure them that there would be no arrests, no "bad publicity."

In one of our core team weekly conference calls, I told my fellow organizers about this concern. They had a good laugh and then said this is because of the two groups leading this rally. They were NCIL and another predominantly "stick it to The Man group," ADAPT. In 2011, there was a serious divide between these organizations, even though they were part of the disability rights community. Regardless of that, the My Medicaid Matters Rally was a huge success.

That split between CCD and NCIL and ADAPT would be put on hold in the wee hours of the morning of November 9, 2016. It was time for solidarity in the work because we had to prepare for the fight of our lives against a despot who was going to be president of the United States and the Republican-led 115th Congress.

———

In this new position I had a portfolio that consisted of twelve policy issue areas—ADA/civil rights, appropriations and budget, education, employment, financial security, housing, international, Social Security, technology and telecommunications, transportation, veterans affairs, and voting rights. The term *portfolio* in this position refers to a range of issues that a public policy staffer works on through coalitions, on the Hill, and with the administration. Most importantly for NCIL, the work is directed by those with lived experience or those directly impacted. This was my opportunity to branch out into multiple task forces other than the Education TF within CCD. We were also a member of the Leadership Conference, so I was able to branch out into multiple issue areas in that space, like census data, the courts, education and transportation equity, hate and bias, immigration, justice reform, and LGBTQ equality. The board and staff members embraced my work on criminal and juvenile justice, and I returned to that collaborative work as well.

By now I was entering my third year in the disability rights community, working on a grant program and now finally able to do policy work. Many in CCD had never met me because I had not been at the policy task-force meetings.

There is nothing like first impressions. You don't get a chance to change that first interaction. They say that the first thing a bird sees is its mother and that image is imprinted on its mind forever. I wanted my entrance into this community to be one that they would never forget but most of all respect. It's not a part of my nature to desire to be embraced or to seek acceptance.

I learned in my career pathway training back in the corporate world that when you go on an interview remember that not only are you being interviewed for the position, but you want to interview them for your goals. They taught us to walk around the offices and observe who works for the company. Do the people in the office look like you? Are there women in positions you want to hold? When you are asked do you have any questions of us, be prepared with at least one or two about the company and its work.

These trainings were created by and presented to white workers. I would always bring to the attention of all in the room that I have never gone to an office and found someone who looks like me doing what I want to do. I am breaking a ceiling, so what type of questions do I ask? If I set this as a standard for taking a position, I would never have entered the field. Each trainer I encountered at these sessions would nod their head in affirmation but never offer suggestions or tools for improving my career journey—that of a Black woman. It was beyond frustrating, but I again honed in on my talent for finding a solution from another source.

I took that training for improving my career into policy work. Most meetings for the TFs were held at the offices of the cochairs for the issue area, such as the Rights TF monthly meeting, which was held at the offices of those cochairs. We would travel all across DC to attend meetings in-person but there was always the call-in option, which is what the other two people of color policy staffers chose to do.

Upon entering those offices, I went into full interview mode—looked around the offices and see if you see people who look like you. Yes, I did. I saw some Black people in these offices. Those people of color and specifically Black people working in these disability rights organizations usually were in positions of service. They were the receptionists, program managers, or office support staff. Then there were a number of interns or fellows not working on policy and not getting paid. Can you say elitist?

Yes, even in the social justice organizations—specifically in these organizations. It is one of the reasons the conservatives are luring talent. Those conservative organizations provide paid internships and fellowships that are designed to create new opportunities for this new workforce. Social justice organizations say farewell and best wishes to their interns and fellows, for there is little to no place for new talent in these groups. This is even more prominent in the disability rights community. It is difficult to enter a field that has a career span of fifteen to twenty years on average for policy analyst or organizations that just can't afford to expand their policy staff because funders are not willing to provide money for capacity building in the area of lobbying. Lobbying has become a bad word, but there is nothing wrong with lobbying or having this as a primary function of an organization of change. In fact, one of the core factors for change in collective liberation is influencing government action and legislative changes. The oppressors are doing this and doing it well. They provide promising careers with well-paying positions funded by wealthy people who say "go forth and lobby."

There are organizations in DC that have had the same number of policy staff for over thirty years, and that number will not increase because of the lack of serious strategy and funding for policy work; those people will not be leaving their positions any time in the near future.

In corporate America, this would be seen as stagnation, lacking improvement, and harmful to progress. In those spaces, leadership is constantly doing capacity building and looking for new talent to bring innovation to the team. The lack of resources for increasing staff capacity is one of the reasons used by most disability rights organizations for not hiring more disabled and BIPOC people to be part of their policy teams. Another is "we try but we just can't find them." This justification continues to be used to this day.

———

My daily routine working for NCIL included attending CCD TF meetings, because that is where the work is done, and this quickly became mentally and emotionally harmful to me. Although I was in my third year of this work, this was my first time at these meetings. I had to prove that I had expertise and knew what I was talking about, as is expected of all new people in organizations. My master's in public administration and seven years of policy experience was not enough to pass the test. Time and time again I had to prove myself in this work. It was not that I had to prove that I could do the work, but I had to prove that I could work within the boundaries set forth by the leadership.

At first I thought that these white leaders were aware of their constricting practices and even more of their privilege. But as the weeks moved on it became clearer to me that these people knew little about coalition work outside of CCD and that they functioned within the constructs of power that perpetuated the old guard. Any new ideas or any new people who tried to enter the conversation were met with intimidation. It was subtle but the message was clear: "Do as you are told, not as you wish!"

After three months of this kind of work, I made a decision to find a way to accomplish my goals through other means: process and collaboration. As I did back in my seventh-grade class when my teacher would not answer my questions, I found other ways to achieve my goal of creating policy that would improve lives.

The first thing I did was concede my lack of knowledge. I have a lot of education, but in every position you enter there is "on the job training" that only experience can teach you. In this policy position I realized that I knew the theory of the functions of the three branches of government. Of course I did, as I was a political science major and policy nerd at a very young age. But what I lacked knowledge in was the actual functions of each branch and, of course, the politics of how they worked. At this time I was not a policy wonk, and I had to become one and fast.

How do you learn this? Is there a course you take to learn this process? If so, does this mean I have to go back to school? I didn't learn what I needed in all of that education? Who do I go to, to find my answers?

OK, I must take a moment here to discuss my concerns with these descriptions of my home. Forgive me, but my heart will not let me move forward without doing this. DC is not a state, a city, a town, or a municipality as defined in the public administration and urban planning policies. It is the District of Columbia. I am a proud member of the Neighbors United for DC Statehood group. We are a neighborhood grassroots organization with presence in all eight wards that works through education, advocacy, and lobbying for the independence of our seven hundred thousand neighbors to obtain statehood.

I called DC a place for the masters of the game. What does that mean? Well, one thing masters don't do is ask questions or show weakness by admitting ignorance. Part of the DC culture is that everybody here knows everything all the time. It is annoying at times and in my opinion downright harmful to the work. Because of this, I knew that I was going to have to be a different kind of policy analyst in the disability rights community. I was going to have to be an activist first.

Activists are lifelong learners. I took on my first challenge and began to learn how the three branches of government worked. What does it mean to lobby? Now, I had a bit of this education from my first contractual position in DC. But that was only for a short stint, and I was mostly doing program grant work. I made another promise to myself: When I am in a room and they are discussing something that is unknown to me, I will ask questions. I continuously said to myself, "Don't be afraid to admit not knowing because you are not here for you! Dara, you are here and others are not. Use that privilege and get something done."

Then I used those keen traits of analysis and inquisitiveness to seek out those who were knowledgeable in how the three branches worked. There are some "smart ass" people in DC. They are usually the quiet ones, but not always. When a meeting ended I would go over to those in the room who impressed me with their knowledge and ask them if we could have coffee. Now the coffees, drinks, and dinners became education and, at the same time, bonding sessions.

Some of those people remain mentors, educators, and dear friends to this day.

I learned about "The Hill." Just knowing that terminology is a DC thing. "The Hill" is a term used by lobbyists, policy staff, reporters, and many others to refer to the US Congress, on Capitol Hill. "I will be on the Hill all day tomorrow." When stating this, one could be on the House or Senate side and in some cases in the US Capitol meeting usually with staff or actual members of Congress. I am blessed to meet with actual members from time to time. I have been in a room multiple times, in the US Capitol, in leadership's chambers with about six other Congress members in attendance discussing strategy either to stop or win an upcoming imperative vote. Believe me, I constantly pinch myself when I leave those meetings and say, "Yes you are living this life!" Then I get to work!

Over a few months I learned from very smart fellow policy analysts, Hill staffers, and anyone else who would talk to me about how Congress works. Not the politics of Congress, as that is something different. That is *how do you get* things done in Congress? I learned the functions of Congress. This is *how things are done* in Congress? One way is to have the right tools. There is a book that you must have and keep on you at all times. The person who showed it to me called it their bible. This book is a directory and titled *The Original U.S. Congress Handbook.*

I did not know about this book and its importance in assisting me to be an effective policymaker. The *Handbook*, which is updated yearly, provides me with a plethora of information about members, their office location, phone number, staff members, committee assignments, and so much more. It is a tool that I don't go without in my work. I purchase two each session, one for home and one that never leaves my bag.

When I am on the Hill or in meetings around town I have that book along with a copy of the US Constitution. Why? Because often even people on the Hill will tell you something is in the Constitution or refer to language they think is in the document. Being the smartass I can be, when I think what they are saying is b.s., I pull it out and say "Really, where exactly is that written in the Constitution?"

My expert teachers became friends and often told me how they loved my desire to learn and my open ability to come to them with inquiries. It was refreshing to get to know these people on another level. Yes, they were mostly white people, but there were a few people of color doing policy in DC.

I have learned that I am a person who feeds off of energy. My parents and friends tell me all the time that I have an infectious smile and a wonderful spirit that is welcoming and inviting to those with the symbiotic vibe. These teachers were definitely providing me with knowledge not only about the workings of Congress but with history about the work. I learned a lot about the disability rights movement from those who were there. It was like when I attend my sorority and church conferences or events and sat with the "seasoned" folk to hear the stories of how it was for the movement.

The lessons included the importance of knowing about committees, co-sponsorships, hearings vs. briefings vs. mark-ups, redlining a bill, and so much more. They taught me that working on the Hill was done best by those who could develop relationships. They told me that if you can be a good friend to staff, be honest, follow through, and provide them with good information from time to time, you will be a great policymaker.

One of my mentors, a phenomenal Black woman civil rights activist and former director of the DC ACLU policy office, Laura Murphy, taught me to be bipartisan in my work. She taught me to work with both parties and get to know all staffers on committees. The goal is to get the job done, and on the Hill it takes both parties. She told me that staffers may not want to meet with you, but you should use the membership of your organization to get in the door, then impress them with your work ethic, and they will respect you. They may not be on your side, but they will assist you where they can. These are words that have been of exponential assistance to me as a policymaker. It was also a different political era in the early 2000s, when I was learning this, but I continue to be bipartisan in my work even in these polarizing times.

Building relationships was a no-brainer to me. I was created and put on earth for this, and it is what has made me such an effective policymaker. I truly enjoy working with staff on the Hill, and it has been one of the highlights of my career to attend multiple signing ceremonies at the White House as the president of the United States signs a bill that we all worked on into law.

———

When a bill is introduced into Congress, I learned, there is much work to be done by those advocates supporting the bill and those who oppose. It goes to the committee of jurisdiction, which means it gets worked on and has movement or is stifled and stalled. Bills can and often do get sent to multiple committees because the language covers multiple areas of concern. An example is mental health legislation, which often is worked on by multiple committees because of the areas of expertise that need to be addressed.

I worked on a large (omnibus) mental health bill passed at the very end of the 114th Congress in December 2016. It was the first time in about fifteen years that there had been any overhaul of legislation for mental health services. This was a battle to get much of this bill revamped and language removed or changed, as when it was originally written the language was quite harmful to the civil and human rights of persons with mental health diagnosis. But the bills were in multiple committees of jurisdiction because of the structure of the chambers (House and Senate).

In the 114th the Republicans had control of both chambers, which had not happened since the 109th Congress (2005–2007). Having control of both chambers means that party has the power and chairs all committees of jurisdiction on legislation. They decide which legislation advances to votes or gets stalled and left in committee going nowhere. In this case there was bipartisan desire to get a mental health bill passed, so this legislation got plenty of movement. In the House, the bill went to one committee of jurisdiction (Energy and Commerce), and in the Senate the bill was sent to two committees of jurisdiction because of the language. The health and clinical section of the bill was handled in the Health, Education, Labor, and Pensions Committee (HELP). Then, because of the financial implications in the bill (Medicaid), the legislation also went to the Finance Committee for jurisdiction oversight.

Once the bills pass out of their committees of jurisdiction, which is no easy task and can take years, sometimes multiple congressional terms, they are sent to the floor for a full chamber vote. The Congressional Research Office reports that the average time for a bill to pass today is eight Congresses, that is sixteen years. The Equality Act, which is introduced in every Congress, the civil rights bill for LGBTQIA+ community has been worked on for fifty-plus years.

This mental health legislation was worked on for three terms (112th, 113th, and 114th Congresses). The bills then go to a full floor vote in each chamber. Sometimes bills get added to other bills that are passing. This mental health bill was completed this way. The Helping Families in Mental Health Crisis Act language was added to the 21st Century Cures Act passed in December 2016. The work of the coalition I led dismantled a number of harmful amendments and provisions and helped pass a bill with better programs, services, and funding. It also saved the Protection and Advocacy for Individuals with Mental Illness (PAIMI) civil rights program.

Hopefully, buy-in and support conversations with the White House have been completed prior to the bill being passed in both chambers, something usually done by Congress and advocates. I have had many meetings with White House staff about legislation that activists support and oppose. This is part of the job of being a good federal policy analyst and activist in DC. The president's support of legislation can be imperative to its movement in Congress. In the case of the mental health bill, President Obama was in support of both the Cures and the Helping Families Act.

Once the bills pass the chambers they are sent to the White House. There is the ceremony at the White House or some other venue around DC where the president of the United States uses multiple pens to sign that legislation you helped to get passed. The written legislation for which you coordinated advocates from around the nation to support and did the political and policy work on the Hill to get done is now public law.

Then I learned that passing a bill is not the end of the work; in most cases it is only the beginning. After learning about how the Hill functions, this was my second lesson in doing the work of becoming a better policy analyst. In activism you push for legislative change, and once the bill is passed, most activists move on to the next bill to be passed. But there is an entire process for getting that legislative language executed and enforced by government entities. The second chamber of government is the administration. It is imperative to being a good policymaker to have great relationships with the White House and administration offices for completing the work.

I attend high-level meetings with members of most administrative departments to discuss the implementation of recently as well as long ago passed bills. The Americans with Disabilities Act (ADA) was passed in 1990, yet we are still waiting for regulations to be done for some of the law. This is over thirty years later, and they still have not been completed. Creating, writing, and implementing regulations are the other side of policy work—some say the boring side. It is work left to "the experts" in this town, mostly the lawyers, who are all white. But it would behoove many activists to become immersed in this work as this is where "the rubber meets the road," as they say.

I am sure that many activists had never heard of the regulation process or rules or guidance prior to the 2016 election. It was apparent when many inquired about this process and I was a part of multiple training calls and conversations once the #45 administration started reneging and pulling a number of crucial civil rights guidances. This is what I think of as being "woke" when the term is used. The election of a despot gave this country an injection of knowledge about how the government functioned and the importance of who is the president of these here United States and what that means to the movement.

The regulatory process is one that is of importance to the work and must be preserved for the full implementation of the law. It entails writing comments when the government sends out requests and being involved in the process of implementation for many years. Implementation entails multiple meetings, sometimes for many years with many administrative offices, and advocating for the law to be rolled out correctly. This is another area for which progressive and liberal social justice organizations need funding to hire competent and great talent to accomplish their goals. But because this is also considered lobbying, because the process includes influencing the government, many funders will not provide funding for regulatory work. It entails direct communication and working with the administration and Congress. There are educated, trained, and talented people ready to do this work. But because there is a lack of funding, the opportunities are few and far between. The lack of funding for this work creates more suffering and is unproductive for the movement of transformative change.

The final area of work that I needed some on the job training was in the judiciary, the third branch of government. As a policy analyst who is not an attorney, I do not have much experience in this field. But I, of course, work with many legal eagles and read many cases for research and to get information for the policy work. I know that litigation work is important for the cause, but it is not my priority. I also don't uphold the DC civil rights organizations' attitude that embodies the idea of worshipping the courts as the most important place to fight our fight. I am of the mindset of Michelle Alexander and her writing about litigation in her amazing book *The New Jim Crow*:

> In recent years, however, a bit of mythology has sprung up regarding the centrality of litigation to racial justice struggles. The success of the brilliant legal crusade that led to *Brown v. Board of Education* has created a widespread perception that civil rights lawyers are the most important players in racial justice advocacy. . . . As public attention shifted from the streets to the courtroom, the extraordinary grassroots movement that made civil rights legislation possible faded from public view. The lawyers took over.
>
> With all deliberate speed, civil rights organizations became "professionalized" and increasingly disconnected from the communities they claimed to represent.[1]

I learned much later that many of the lawyers I was working with in DC also had no formal education on public policy process or disability law. This is a community that learns on the job. There is a group of people who have been doing this for years who pass the torch. This lack of knowledge provided through formal education is another form of blocking talent. When policy positions open in the disability community, there is an expectation that the person filling the position has some working knowledge of how the Hill functions and of disability rights and laws. It is almost impossible to prove that if you have not been formally immersed in this work prior to applying for the open position. This is where privilege, and in the disability rights community, white nondisabled privilege, rears its ugly head by keeping those not privy to this type of training or connections out of the process.

Those classes at my esteemed alma mater were amazing, but they did not instruct me in disability law. One of my tasks at NCIL was to staff a few of the subcommittees for the legislative and advocacy work at my new organization. The subcommittees are led by NCIL members who volunteer their time and expertise in the subject matter to move the policy agenda. I was working at a member-driven disability rights organization. What does that mean? In this organization there are policies stating that the leadership of the organization (the board) will be completely made up of people with disabilities, the staff will consist of no less than 51 percent of people with disabilities, the members will vote for the leadership of the organization and will drive the policy agenda and legislative and advocacy work through surveys, and no work will be conducted without the input of the members.

One of these subcommittees is the ADA/civil rights group, where the members work on protecting this amazing civil rights law. There has been a consistent push from a few in the business community to weaken this law and stop many of its rules and regulations from being issued and published by the government. There is a rule set forth by the co-chairs of the committee that members must be well versed in the ADA. NCIL made each member learn the law and take a test through a program titled ADA Basic Building Blocks. It is a series of tests that one can take for free and on their own time. Members are required to score 85 percent or better, but this was loosely implemented. The chairs really wanted people to look at the law and know the basics.

The first time I was on the monthly call for the ADA/ CR subcommittee, one of the cochairs asked me if I had taken my test. I had not but was eager to do so. The logic behind making each member learn the ADA and take this test was pretty basic. How can you fight for your rights if you don't know your rights? I looked at my plans and said how can I make policy change and not know the basic law of disability rights?

I set out to learn all I could about disability laws. In the TF meetings that I attended here in DC, I heard terms I really did not understand. Many were discussing how a program or an institution was "ignoring Section 504." In DC policy work we speak in acronyms and about laws and policies as if all in the room are "in the know." I had no idea what section 504 was, and I stopped the conversation to ask, "What is 504?"

It was apparent that I had flustered some and aggravated others. These white privileged people were used to working in spaces where all of their fellow white colleagues had the knowledge they needed to do the work. I was blessed to have a few people who I could go to after the meetings and get information from them. Just like I did back in elementary school to get answers from my teacher, I found another means to the end. They provided me with explanations, resources, and, best of all, kindness, which is a rarity in the disability rights community.

I set out to learn all I could about disability rights laws and those laws that support or can be used in conjunction with them to protect the civil and human rights of the disabled. This would allow me to become an expert in the field and at the same time increase my ability to create better legislative language on disability policy issues. I continued to be a thorn in their side, as I did not stop asking questions, and the more knowledge I gained, the more of "a problem" I became to the disability rights community. The W. E. B.

Du Bois question *"How does it feel to be a problem?"* continued to move my soul to know that being a problem for this community was an absolute right and, dare I say, an obligation to my people.

———

This was the start of a long and continuous road of educating, training, and learning about not only disability rights laws but the history around how and why they were created. Every other year I attend training sessions on the ADA at conferences. It is part of my commitment to be a lifelong learner. Back then I set out to learn about the history and the laws that were created prior to the ADA. In my trainings around the country and as a scholar teaching public policy, I relay what I have learned about this and its significance to the creation of public policy. What I learned reading about the statutes was amazing, but the stories around them are fascinating and completely white, as if no other race of people assisted with the passage of this historic law.

The ADA did not just happen one day, and there were other laws that preceded its creation. Many talk about how the ADA created accessible entrances, doorways, and bathrooms for the disabled. This is true, but this is not the premise of the ADA, nor is it the reason for this civil rights legislation. In my trainings, education sessions, and speeches, I tell people that when it comes to disabilities, if they understand anything let it be these two things: One, there is nothing wrong with having a disability. Two, the premise of the ADA is community integration. I also discuss equity and that being anti-racist is not enough; I need them to be pro-Black in the work of creating public policy.

I always start my presentations with the Architectural Barriers Act of 1968 (ABA), the statute that stipulates accessible entrances, doorways, and such things. This law remains on the books and is enforced by the US Access Board, a federal agency tasked with setting the standards for this law as well as many others things around accessibility in this country. The board decides how wide a doorway has to be in order to be accessible. The ABA created a pathway into a building for the disabled but did not provide them with a civil right. Here is a hypothetical example: There is a student who uses a wheelchair and wants to attend university classes. That student may have been able to get into the classroom had this university created ramps, wider entrance doors, and hallways. But once in the classroom the professor could and some did say, "You in the wheelchair, get out of my class! I am not teaching anyone like you!" The person had to leave. Why? Because they had no civil right that provided them with the protection to remain in the classroom and force the professor to instruct them along with all the other students.

In 1973, the Rehabilitation Act was passed. This law has multiple sections of importance in the protection of the rights of the disabled: Section 501 covers employment, 503 prohibits federal contractors from discriminating against the disabled, 504 prohibits any program receiving federal funding from discriminating against the disabled, and 508 covers technology, websites, etc.

What did this law do in my scenario? That student in the wheelchair could now get into the university classroom and the professor had to instruct them. There is no higher education program in the country that does not receive federal funding, as they all get some type of research grant, have highways and byways that come through campus, etc., so in some way, Section 504 covers the disabled in those institutions. This student was integrated into the educational system but could be and was excluded from social interactions. The students leave class through the accessible doorways and go down the ramp and decide they want to eat at a restaurant not owned by the university.

They cross the street and now this student in the wheelchair runs into barriers, such as there is no ramp and definitely the doorway is not wide enough for them to enter. The owner of the restaurant says, "We don't serve people like that in our establishment!" Their fellow students push back and say, "No, they must be able to eat with us here." The owner replies, "I don't have to serve this person and you can't make me!"

This part about denying disabled people services happened, and unfortunately, thirty-plus years out from passage of the ADA, it continues to happen to the disabled. In 1973, even with the Rehab Act, the restaurant owner did not have to serve the student in the wheelchair because the eatery was not receiving federal funds. The student did not have civil rights in that restaurant because the ADA was not a federal law.

Now, my scenario is not complete without discussing that in fact there probably were few to no students in wheelchairs going to a university. It was not until 1975 that the Individuals with Disabilities Education Act (IDEA) was passed. This law provides that students with disabilities receive a Free Appropriate Public Education. This covers elementary and secondary school, though, not higher education. This law is supposed to create inclusive education for students with disabilities and provide them with the services they need to be in class. Forty-plus years later we continue to fight the battle to implement IDEA in this country. In fact, discrimination in educational institutions for students with disabilities remains on the forefront of the fight for community integration. The other push is for any White House administration to put in its budget and for Congress to fully fund IDEA. This funding needs to be at a level that will provide the much-needed resources for educators and providers of imperative services such as PT, OT, etc., for students with disabilities.

In 1986, Congress passed the Air Carrier Access Act (ACAA). This law was sponsored by Senator Robert Dole (R-KS) with a big advocacy push by a veterans' organization to get this done. ACAA is about one page long and it covers airlines and planes from the opening of the gate, the gateway to the plane, and the plane itself. If you have been on a plane in the last few years you see that this law remains something that we work on to get fully implemented as well. The planes remain inaccessible, as do most of the services on them, such as the bathrooms, announcements, and movies.

Just think that when the flight attendants do their instructions at the beginning of the journey, if you have a person who is Deaf or hard of hearing sitting next to you, they are missing out on that entirely. Not so annoying now, is it? If there is an emergency during the flight and the captain interrupts the communications system to give an announcement, that same person is again left out of the notification. There are no ASL interpreters on the plane and no captioning going across a screen to inform them of the same information you just received.

But activists continuously work with the airline industry, government, and others to get to a place of full accessibility. We also work on strengthening the ACAA, for there is no private right of action in the statute. This means that people do not have the right to sue the airline; so what happens? There is a complaint process set up by the government, specifically the Department of Transportation (DOT). Those who have issues during their flying experience file complaints, and

DOT follows up with warnings to the airlines. If there are too many of the same complaints for the same airlines, this is called an established pattern of practice and DOT will address this with that airline. Hence the work we are doing to strengthen this law.

In 1990, the Americans with Disabilities Act (ADA) was passed. There is a long history about this process and the advocacy plan around how this became a law. The history put forth by the disability rights community is completely white and lacks any discussion, description, or accolades of BIPOC, LGBTQIA+, or other disenfranchised people who participated in creating this legislation. It is only in recent years, because historians called it out, that some in the disability rights community have admitted that there were people from multi-marginalized groups who contributed to the advocacy work of this historic law. It was the fiftieth anniversary of the Black Panthers that educated many on the fact that Black people in DC assisted the disability rights community on the famous Crawl protest that was done March 12, 1990.

The ADA created a civil right for the disabled. Now the student in the wheelchair could attend the university and have fun with their fellow students at any restaurant around campus. The first part of this scenario that is imperative to the conversation is that this person in a wheelchair was actually living in the community. The premise of the ADA is community integration.

When I do my discussions on these laws, one of my pretest questions is, Has anyone heard of the Ugly Laws? I usually get blank stares and maybe one person will say yes. This is even in 2022, as this history remains out of the mainstream conversations of most who work on disability issues. They do not make the connection of community integration, because these privileged white disability rights advocates are not advocating for the end to the institutionalization of people into mental health facilities, nursing homes, jails, prisons, and other institutions. This is not on many of their policy agendas.

The Ugly Laws of 1865 were first introduced to the world in the "liberal" city of San Francisco. These laws basically said that if a person had a disability, they could not be in public spaces. They could not attend school, go to the park, go to an amusement park, go to the grocery store, or go to a house of worship. These laws were created and implemented around the world and remain on the books in a number of countries to this day.

Then, in 1935, the racist and ableist Franklin D. Roosevelt (FDR) decided to codify these Ugly Laws, and instead of keeping these disabled people in your home, he created the institutionalization of disabled people. Yes, FDR was a person with a disability, but he hid it from many and he was not born with his disability. Also, the fact that someone has a disability does not mean they acknowledge this fact or believe in the civil and human rights of people with disabilities.

The codification of the idea of Ugly Laws with the New Deal's Social Security legislation started the practice of babies who were born with disabilities or young children who were diagnosed with disabilities being thrown into institutions. The premise of Ugly Laws was that the disabled could not be seen in public, so instead of keeping them home the government threw them into institutions. Many parents were told by professionals like doctors and social workers that their child would never be able "to live a normal life" and the best place for them was an institution. This practice remains active in the US today. Many families continue to fight to get their children removed from these horrific institutions and brought home.

This community of people had no rights and were abused, neglected, and even tortured in these places. The investigative reporter Geraldo Rivera's first big story was the Willowbrook institution, where he had a doctor wear a pin camera and video the atrocities and helped to close down this horrific facility.

The ADA is the law set forth to dismantle this oppressive, abusive, and disgusting system by creating a pathway to community integration. It is an excellent law but was a compromise and is "the floor." There is more legislation that needs to be passed to accomplish full community integration for all disabled people. These things were promised to disabled people and here it is thirty-plus years later and this promise remains unfulfilled.

———

In addition to examining the laws, I discuss the different methods of addressing disability rights. There are three main "avenues" of how disability rights are viewed and worked on by organizations. They are paternalism, clinical, and civil rights. The first two are driven by ableism, prejudice, and bigotry. Paternalism is the feeling of "Who are they? We have to take care of these people because they can't think for or take care of themselves."

Family groups are usually paternalistic in their advocacy for disabled people. These groups remain powerful and are quite active on the Hill. They are mainly groups that do not fully embrace the ADA as a civil right and continuously place barriers to dismantle the law. They don't believe that all disabled people can and should live on their own.

The argument I use is that it is your family's business how you handle disabilities. But when your views come outside of your family nucleus and interfere with someone else's bodily autonomy, then there are problems. It amazes many when people of prominence in the progressive movement who fought like hell for *Roe v. Wade* and bodily autonomy are not only part of paternalist groups but are leaders serving on the boards. They fight for the civil and human rights of other multi-marginalized groups like LGBTQIA+ people, immigrants, and even the formerly incarcerated, but when it comes to disability issues, they just don't have the same values about or passion for the independent living of disabled people.

Many "progressives" tout their support for civil, human, and environmental rights for all, yet when it comes to the disabled they turn their backs and do horrible things to this community. One such example happened in February 2018, when there were twelve House Democrats who voted in favor of H.R. 620, the ADA Education and Reform Act of 2017. This was legislation set forth to weaken the ADA as a civil right.

Three House Democratic representatives, Jackie Speier, Ami Bera, and Scott Peters, all from California, coauthored this bill with a then prominent Republican House Judiciary Committee member, Ted Poe of Texas. These three House Dems were responsible for garnering at least eighteen other Democrats to cosponsor this bill. When members do this, they are telling leadership—in that year Minority Leader Nancy Pelosi (D-CA)—that they supported the bill and in essence weakening the ADA. Their co-sponsorship indicated that should this bill go to a House floor vote, they would vote yes. When this vote went to a full House floor vote on February 13, 2018, twelve Democrats voted yes for the weakening of the ADA. They were given the title of "The Dirty Dozen" and we called them out on their double standard for not protecting the civil and human rights of the disabled.

It is this type of legislative work that makes people wonder what the difference is between the Republican Party and the Democratic Party. These lines get more and more blurred. Like in the fight to protect the ADA, why is a known human rights activist like Representative Speier not only supporting but coauthoring a bill that will weaken the civil rights of people with disabilities? At the time she was a member of the Congressional Progressive and Equality Caucuses, where she was a staunch supporter of LGBTQIA+ rights. Why would that passion not be extended to protect people with disabilities? This ability to pick and choose what groups of people's rights you protect or to push for political power rather than protect rights is a huge problem even for Democrats. It is a problem when white policymakers in DC continuously assume that Democrats are always on the right side and refer to them as "our friends" when this is not always the case, especially for BIPOC activists. It is why many like myself in the fight for Black liberation and the creation of a new world order continue to push for the end of the binary dichotomy and the creation of new multiple parties.

After paternalism, the second avenue is clinical: "We can cure these people, because there is something wrong!" "Clinicians are going to 'fix' this community." Now don't get me wrong; if a person has a disease that is going to kill them, the movement is all for curing. But there are centers and facilities that believe they can use conversion therapy to shock or remove the disability from a person, no matter the disability. This therapy was done first and adopted by other groups to use in "ending unwanted behaviors" like being LGBTQIA+. The thought that you can "shock" the disability out of someone or control the behavior of the disability is what these therapies claim to accomplish. One such place is the Judge Rotenberg Educational Center in Massachusetts. The United Nations has called shock therapy torture, yet it continues to be used on children and youth right here in the United States. The Obama administration had an opportunity to end shock therapy in the Rotenberg Center but decided not to release this healthcare rule. Advocates across the country remain vigilant about getting this done and closing such centers.

In addition to the subject of how students with disabilities are being treated in educational systems is a form of torture that we fight to dismantle: the restraint and seclusion of students with disabilities. If you know anyone who has a child with a disability and they are sending them to school, tell them to never include restraint and seclusion in their Individual Education Plan.

We have passed laws that say you are not supposed to restrain or seclude people in medical (hospital) settings or juvenile punitive settings. But you can do this to children in a school, the place that is supposed to be the safest setting for them. We all know that being safe in school is over for so many reasons and most definitely for BIPOC students.

Remember the images from Texas in June 2015, when a police officer held down a young Black teenage girl by placing his knee in her back as she was thrown out of a neighborhood pool party by angry white members of that community? That is a form a restraint used on students with disabilities in the classroom by teachers, administrators, law enforcement, and other adults in the school.

There are seclusion boxes in schools around the country. Students with disabilities are sent to those boxes, no reason needed, sometimes for the entire school day. Activists continue to fight this through policy, as there must be a federal law passed to end restraint and seclusion. Currently there is work being done in Congress with the assistance of a number of coalitions. But the push for a federal law has been going on for well over forty years. The largest barrier to this legislation not getting passed is unfortunately the teachers' unions. They have decided that it is a necessity for the safety of the school staff that restraint and seclusion remain part of the standard operating procedure for students with disabilities. They have created barriers and stopped the movement of these bills for over thirty years, although many of the union members and chapters have said they do not agree and would like to see an end to this horrible practice of restraint and seclusion of all students.

As I discussed, there are many "progressives" who claim to be fighting for justice for all, but when it comes to disabled people and issues there is a disconnect. This problem exists with unions in multiple areas. The summer of 2020 and the Black Lives Matter protests proved this when it was disclosed that many unions not only support but housed law enforcement unions within their structures. The reason the AFL-CIO building in DC, located a block from the White House, was trashed and set on fire, as seen on multiple news outlets, was because law enforcement unions had offices in their building. These are the same unions that have a vast majority of members who are BIPOC. Many of their members are Black and were in the streets demanding that law enforcement, protected by these unions, stop killing their people.

Another area in clinical disability work is in gene therapy. There are countries that are working on creating gene therapy to remove the possibility of people having babies born with intellectual and developmental disabilities. In disability justice there is no judgment of how people decide to have a family, and the decisions they make in creating it as long as they are not harming others in the process. This goes back to bodily autonomy. What cannot be tolerated as a society is the state having the power to tell people what type of families they can create, the government telling people there will be no disabled people born in this country. This is well beyond what civil and human rights activists should accept from any power structure.

The third avenue of working disability issues is civil and human rights. It is also the most controversial area because many believe in paternalism and that disabled people do not have the ability to think for themselves. The work of creating civil rights for disabled people is hindered because there is enormous pushback and denial from people with archaic and antiquated thoughts about disability. Many still believe in the premise of the Ugly Laws of 1865. The image and concept of disability remains one of devaluing the lives of disabled people. The work of disability as a civil and human right, through the lens of Black liberation, must be at the forefront of creating change.

Society must believe that all people with disabilities can and should live in the community and not in institutions. This has been upheld in the US Supreme Court with the case of *Olmstead v. Lois Curtis*. Disabled people should be provided with supports and given opportunities to decent and safe education, employment, housing, and all aspects of life.

Each one of us needs supports to survive. Those supports just look and may even function differently for disabled people. But they should not hinder their ability to not only live but thrive in the community.

———

Many don't know that the federal government and faith-based organizations are exempt from the ADA, but not from the ABA or Section 504 of the Rehab Act. It is a shame that even today the United States Capitol and both the House and Senate buildings that I hold sacred to my work continue to have accessibility issues for the disabled.

Yes there are ramps and doors for the entrances, but there is no Braille on buildings, elevators, or doorways for members' offices. Those who are blind or have low vision have a difficult time navigating what building, floor, or even office they are visiting because there are no markings for them. If you have ever attended or watched a hearing, mark-up, or briefing in Congress, you will note that not all provide ASL interpretation in the room, nor do they have a closed-caption crawl across the broadcast for those watching on screens, and they usually do not provide large-print or Braille documents in the room or online. Many congressional offices have websites and post documents that are inaccessible to some of their constituents.

This lack of accessibility leaves out a large number of the disabled because many use ASL and closed captioning. It is not just for those who are Deaf or hard of hearing. People with developmental disabilities, learning disabilities, and mental health diagnoses, as well as other disabilities, rely upon ASL and/or closed captioning as their primary form of communication.

This is disrespectful to an entire community that is active in the political process and has the civil right to have these services provided to them as they visit and interact with those in the US Capitol. The Office of Congressional Accessibility Services, in the Capitol, continues to work on this issue thirty-plus years after the ADA and forty-plus years after the ABA and Section 504.

It is amazing that faith-based organizations asked to be exempt from the ADA. The "love thy fellow man (person)" went out the door when it came to this law. This was the conservative Christian crew. It is good to see that many faiths, like other Protestant Christians, AME, Jewish, and Muslim, have done what is called "going above and beyond the law" and incorporated accessibility and inclusion into their work.

———

In the two years that I worked for NCIL, I learned so much about the process of creating policy, disability rights law and history, and how to collaborate to be successful in several policy campaigns. I also had the opportunity to work with advocates from around the country and the world. These relationships are what sustained me. They would be the salvation I needed to continue my activism in disability policy. It was an experience that continues to hold a special place in my heart and was central to my work as an activist and policymaker.

One part of that experience was creating and being a part of panel discussions. I completely understand the power of having a voice on these types of panels and "expert" discussions. Being out in the public and speaking is for the movement of imperative life-changing policy and for the ability to infuse the need for Black Liberation in this work. I set out to make sure that I was on these types of panels consistently in my work. Doing so required a combination of studying and learning my stuff, writing, networking, and something I was blessed with: being a good speaker.

Reflecting back, I see how this work experience foundation and on-the-job training influenced my later work. There are no words to describe the feeling of witnessing the president sign legislation you worked on. I have been working with Congress to pass federal laws since 2004 and have worked on over twenty-five federal bills that have gone to five different presidents' desks—Clinton to Biden. Yes, I even worked on bills that passed and were signed by that despot of a president, #45.

I have worked on projects all of my adult life and when you successfully complete them it feels good. When you work on the legislation from its inception, or even if you come in the middle and work to get it to the finish line, that feeling is elating. There are two parts to this excitement. The first is to sit in the galley in the US Capitol and hear the votes on your bill in both the House and the Senate, as the legislation you worked on receives yea votes to move to success. I get goosebumps writing this. There are US congresspeople voting on language you helped develop, write, and get passed into law.

That was the inside-the-DC-Beltway policy work. My other experience, of being able to remain an organizer through my work in NCIL, was also fulfilling and added to my expertise. I have discussed the My Medicaid Matters Rally of 2011. That was my first campaign and opportunity to create a connection between DC beltway policymakers and around the country advocates. It was difficult and many were not excited about the collaboration with or the processes of the "in the streets" activists. They let me know this, but I ignored their "concerns" and went forward with the plan set forth by those living with disabilities and not these Beltway policy wonks. It was then that I decided to be a different type of DC policy wonk. That seventh grader who found a way around authority was now an adult thriving and one who decided to reject authority and in my opinion incompetence. I had been doing this work for two years and I was sick and tired of "the old guard"—let me rephrase that, "the old white guard"—being in control.

CHAPTER 4

DIRECT WITH GREAT FORCE

I am not sure why my immediate thoughts about engaging in my vow to make a change in disability policy work in DC were optimistic because my past has proven to me that integration is rarely if ever embraced by the majority. But Ida B. Wells said it best: "The way to right wrongs is to turn the light of truth upon them."[1] And, as my nana (my dad's mom) taught me, "Changemakers shake the core, mess things up, and move the needle of power!" They are usually disliked by the majority.

The "pushback" or denial of their superiority is no different in the white disability rights community, specifically in DC, and is true around the country. It is dangerous to the work and to society, to ignore that there are people who have motives outside of any belief in an egalitarian society and are not only at the table but leaders who set the table. "But to deny the dark nature of human personality is not only fatuous but dangerous," said Gore Vidal.[2]

Denying the dark nature of human personality has been dangerous for the disability rights movement in DC for over forty years, which is how long CCD, the largest disability rights coalition in the country, has dominated disability rights, not only in DC (Congress, White House) but also around the country. What do I mean by these assertions?

There are people who claim to be disability rights advocates and doing this work to create better lives for those with disabilities. This may be true for some, but for many this is a career, not a "matter of life and death," and therefore they have no sense of urgency to create change. It is a large group that also doesn't see the need or political value to demand immediate change. Why? Because they profusely wield the belief that they are "good people" who have empathy to always do the right thing (which is questionable) and, even worse, in their own time (which is not immediate).

These types of "advocates" are more concerned about the course of their careers, becoming people of prominence, than the issues and systems that need to be destroyed and dismantled. This was quite obvious during the 2016 election season. Many were vying for positions and laying the groundwork for work in the much-anticipated Hillary Rodham Clinton White House. They had the same lack of political insight that so many in this country had in the fall of 2016.

They were absolutely convinced that the White House would be a Clinton House and the US Senate would be Democratic-led for the 115th Congress. Both assertions turned out to be so wrong, which is also typical of this white disability rights leadership as they lack political savvy. They don't have a read on the country as they work from a space that is narrow, insular, and composed of those they know. The shock of having a despot in the White House remains something many in this world have not come to terms with, may never truly accept, and most assuredly are not ready for with a possible second term.

The "politicos" of the disability rights movement were not only shocked about the 2016 presidential election, but their entire political strategy plan for the 115th Congress went up in flames as well. In my work of doing trainings, speeches, and presentations, I had the ability to travel the country. I was actively and intimately involved in multiple communities. It was in many of those places that I saw the people who would ultimately become the MAGA crew. So, when #45 came down that escalator in NYC in June 2015 and said he would be running for office, I turned to my boss at the time and said, "That is your next president." My boss laughed at me and said I was completely off on this one. I was told by many that I had no idea what I was talking about when I said that the US Senate would remain Republican-led and that Donald Trump would be your next president. (I won several bets on this assertion in 2016.) My being out in the country and not just sitting being in the DC Beltway every day continues to give me a completely different perspective on this country.

The politicos also were in charge of choosing the next congressional disability rights champion after Senator Tom Harkin retired. They chose Democratic senator Bob Casey of Pennsylvania, a white, cisgender, nondisabled man. In a community that is fraught with race and multi-marginalization issues, this is who they chose. But they claim to be committed to racial justice.

Why did they not choose Democratic senator Tammy Duckworth of Illinois, an Asian American, veteran mom with a visible disability to be the next champion for this community? Because as usual those with lived experience with disabilities were not at the decision table and those with the power in this community pushed their agenda for seeking political power and their next career positions, rather than pursuing solidarity and liberation for all. This area of assertion is only one example of how they use power and direct an entire community with great force.

———

When did social justice work become a business? In my multiple conversations with activists around the nation there are thoughts about the "new players" in the criminal justice scene who are using capitalist processes to end mass incarceration. Social justice soldiers believe that there is no way that we are going to end the subjugation of Black and Brown people and racist systems through business models used in capitalist economies. This quote by Audre Lorde—"The master's tools will never dismantle the master's house"[3]—speaks directly to this thought process.

Similarly, this white leadership group in the disability rights community in DC has this political power plan that is elitist and exclusively exploiting disability issues and uses the same capitalist concepts for its outreach in disability policy work. The social definition of capitalism is "survival of the fittest." It is in true form that the leaders of this community "direct with force" for this foundation, as it is the only way in which they know how to thrive.

They have absolutely no strategic plan that encompasses dismantling an oppressive and destructive system that strips away the civil and human rights as they claim. They purposefully push back with disdain and anger on any work that will engage in anti-racism, which also must include being pro-Black. There is no strategy to end homophobia and xenophobia or embrace the formerly incarcerated in disability issues. The approach to transformative justice reform, such as addressing law enforcement killing disabled people, does not include the criminalization of BIPOC disabled. Instead, this work is led by white disabled advocates who center victimization, which embraces the thought that if only law enforcement had better training, they would not harm and kill. These things are not purposefully done. They are like most white people in this country who do not believe in criminalization, which is a system based in racism, as the core of law enforcement harming and killing Black people.

The white disabled own all of the work done and erase the work of BIPOC disabled people around both of the most iconic disability rights work, that of the passage of the Rehabilitation Act of 1973 (Section 504) and the ADA. This manifests in multiple ways. In the presentation of history such as documentaries and books, it is rare if ever that you will see BIPOC disabled represented. Also, when looking at multiple pictures from the era you will see BIPOC disabled purposefully unnamed and unidentified. One example is the Oscar-nominated documentary on Netflix, *Crip Camp: A Disability Revolution*, which is a white-centered account of a movement that erases the contributions of disabled BIPOC.

Another area where this whitewashing plays out in the retelling of disability rights history is in the passage of the Americans with Disabilities Act (ADA). So many in the white disability community take credit—"I helped write the ADA!"; "I wrote the ADA!"; "I was the lead on the passage of the ADA!" This "claim to fame" is more important than completing the work, as it is known that the ADA is the floor. It is the bare minimum compromise that they could get when it was passed in 1990. The promises to go back and strengthen this civil right have been long ignored. The strategic plan of these white disabled "champions" is to better their station in life and their glorified historical memory.

You rarely hear from these white leaders about others in the movement. They don't even acknowledge the struggle and fight of millions of grassroots people whose names you will never know and how their strength and hope were the drive behind the passage of such an historic law. Just listen to or read their speeches during the ADA celebrations over the years. It is rare if you hear any of those receiving awards or speaking at events acknowledge disabled BIPOC people, BIPOC congressional members, or civil rights leaders who were a large part of the work of getting the ADA passed into law. If these words are spoken, it is more than likely coming from a BIPOC disabled person or those who are multi-marginalized, which is seldom if ever is done at these celebrations. They do not celebrate BIPOC people, disabled or nondisabled, at their celebrations.

———

My first year in this work I had the opportunity to celebrate the twentieth anniversary of the ADA. The entire year, many had a buzz about how exciting July, the month the ADA was signed, would be for the community. They talked about the many celebrations that would happen around town with multiple organizations celebrating as well as Congress. The ADA passed in the 101st Congress in 1990 and was signed into law by President George H. W. Bush. It is considered a bipartisan law and so all were celebrating this momentous occasion. Those were different times.

The organization I worked for in 2010 was TASH, and we received a number of invitations to events around DC and as a staff we split those invitations up amongst the office of three. I attended multiple events in a week and this lasted for most of the month of July. I went to the celebration held by the Department of Justice (DOJ), our nation's legal center and the key administrative office to enforce our laws. There is an Office of Disability Rights (ODR) in DOJ that has a staff who works specifically on disability issues and cases. But this DOJ event was hosted by multiple departments that also work on disabilities, like the Office of Civil Rights and Office of Justice Programs (OJP).

By the time I got to DOJ's event celebrating the twentieth anniversary, I had been to multiple administrative departments' similar celebrations. The Department of Health and Human Services, Department of Education, Federal Communications Commission, and Department of Transportation all had full ADA twentieth-anniversary celebrations that included the leadership of the departments. These administration celebrations were in addition to those of the many DC Beltway disability rights organizations that are headquartered in the DC area. By the time I sat in the Great Hall in the Robert F. Kennedy DOJ Building, I had met or heard about the "disability champions" of the ADA, and every person was white. Many of them were celebrated by being honored with an award at these events or those awards were named after them commemorating their work in the passage of the historic law.

I ate from several sheet cakes with writing in icing that revealed the names of most if not all of these "champions" of this work. Each person listed was white—another erasure of the BIPOC community who assisted with the passage of this historic law. The names of Representatives Major Owens (D-New York), Barbara Jordan (D-Texas), John Lewis (D-Georgia), Danny Davis (D-Illinois), and many more prominent Black leaders who assisted with the ADA and should have been there were left off these lists.

Of course, these events followed the DC Beltway pattern of having a panel discussion. This is when experts from the field are usually brought in from around the country, maybe even the world, and placed on a stage for a policy or historical conversation. Always in attendance are disability rights advocates, leadership of the administration, leaders and staff of the disability rights organizations, and of course congressional members, and yet again all white.

These congressional members were usually special guests who did the opening speech prior to the panel discussions or were receiving an award at the celebration. At these events, as is done at most anniversary celebrations of historic civil rights legislation, the community honored those who had passed on but who were still very much a part of the history.

Now, by July 2010 I had been involved in the disability rights community for almost eleven months. When I first came on board at TASH, my executive director gave me a few things to read and I also went to the library and pulled books I thought I should read. There was not much written about the social action history of the work around the ADA. One book that is still a staple and is given to most newcomers to this work is *No Pity: People with Disabilities Forging a New Civil Rights Movement*, by Joe Shapiro.

By the twentieth anniversary of the ADA, I had read this book twice, as this is something I do. I am an avid reader and I love history. My mother and my liberal arts education in both secondary school and college taught me that in order to know people, you must know their history. You must understand where they came from; it will assist you with where they want to go. Their history will also be an insight into who they are, the foundation of their community. This does not mean that their history is their destiny for the future, but as with the history of this nation, the institution of slavery is the epicenter for structural racism and sustains these systems of oppression.

In *No Pity*, Shapiro does an excellent job providing not only a detailed historic review of the work around the passage of the ADA; he also writes about the reason this work was undertaken. Joe works for NPR and is one of the few national reporters covering the disability community. He has a close relationship with many in the movement and remains a relevant person who tells the stories no others will discuss. But—and he and I have discussed this—his perspective is completely a white cisgender disabled perspective, because those are the only people interviewed in the book, and it eliminates the BIPOC and multi-marginalized disabled experience.

In July 2010, I was blessed to have either met or been in the room with most of those people still living who are mentioned in *No Pity*. I also attended advocacy and policy meetings with most of the people both from the Obama administration and Congress. The DOJ event was one of the final events of the twentieth-anniversary celebration. I learned long ago that the best networkers arrive early to events, because that's where the conversations and connections occur. Also in DC, in the aftermath of 9/11, getting through security was always a long process. So I arrived early for the DOJ twentieth-anniversary ADA celebration not only to connect but to get some answers. I was frustrated and a bit perturbed.

I wanted to know what was going on with these celebrations. More than that, I wanted to know why these people in 2010 were comfortable with the fact that at all of these celebrations only white cisgender people were leading and represented. There was no representation of BIPOC people and very few LGBTQIA+ people, those of a different faith other than Christian or Jewish, the formerly incarcerated, immigrants, refugees, and all the other marginalizations on a panel, discussed in the historic retellings, or receiving an award. The panelist identified themselves and their life experiences. Not one of these awards being handed out was named after any person from those multi-marginalized groups. There are no awards named after a BIPOC or multi-marginalized person in the disability rights community, and the presentation of awards to this community is sadly infrequent, even today.

It was as if those communities did not exist in the DC disability rights community. In asking my questions of the fully white community around me, the answers I got were full of hesitations and "oh that's not true." They had puzzled looks of shock when I made it clear to them that in fact this is what was happening in the nation's capital for the twentieth anniversary of the ADA. I quickly learned that the whitewashed history was the strategic erasure of any and all other communities who are a part of the disability rights movement. It was a deed that most in this community did not want to recognize and most definitely did not want to discuss. It was most undeniably exclusion done "direct with great force."

———

In the celebration of the twentieth anniversary of the ADA, another disrespectful action happened that I thought was a bit odd at first, but after discussing it with others, I came to the right conclusion that this was in fact offensive or rude. The disability rights community has a practice of engaging in patronizing racist and anti-Black comparisons. I thought that these racist comparisons were started by well-meaning people who were ignorant. But yet again, I learned that this is a group of people who are involved in entirely white spaces and engaged in the erasure of BIPOC communities from the history of disability, and none of this can be blamed on ignorance.

The disability rights community continues to call out how they are constantly left out of other rights movements. There is truth to that, but as the saying goes, "Clean your own house before you go trying to clean others'." The disability rights community has a serious issue with the erasure of other rights movements and not including multi-marginalized policy issues in its strategy for policy work. Yet that is never discussed or addressed except in the form of writing a grant to get funds from philanthropic entities. This is a space where white disability rights organizations continue to falsely spout their commitment to anti-racist and pro-Black work.

This is where they, like many others in social justice work, make statements about how they are trying to employ diversity, equity, and inclusion to make change. They use terms like "racial equity," "Intersectionality," and "inclusion" as catchphrases to get the prize. It is highly offensive to those of us who live this every day and see these critical race frames as our lifeline in the work of not only creating a better world for our people but also literally surviving. These are not some words we use to get accolades and prizes in the form of philanthropic funding. We are demanding a new world order, the end of trauma and violence to our communities in multiple forms of reparations, and a systemic change of collective liberation now!

In fact, many in the white disability rights community have contempt for those of us who call them out on a daily basis for their disingenuous work. They do not know or care to know that there is a difference between inclusion and equity. In fact, many who do social justice work do not comprehend or accept this fact, which is one of the many reasons why numerous well-funded programs to create better outcomes are not working.

Many in the white disability rights community refer to the similarities and overlapping of the Black experience to their white disability rights conquest. It is infuriating to constantly fight with this community about the disrespect and intentional harm this does not only to disabled Black people but to all Black people. For example, the disability rights community will compare the SCOTUS case *Brown v. Board of Education* to the *Olmstead v. Lois Curtis* case. They'll compare The Crawl to Selma (Bloody Sunday). A particularly egregious example is the May 2008 article by Richard Holicky, "Escaping the Nursing Home" in *New Mobility* magazine, about deinstitutionalization that used the Underground Railroad as symbolism for disabled people escaping institutions.

It has been explained by many anti-racist, pro-Black BIPOC activists that these comparisons are not only racist, patronizing, and anti-Black but also insulting and out of place in a movement dedicated to creating a new world order. Black liberation and abolitionist as well as other BIPOC activists do not engage in comparisons in the work of collective liberation. But as I have written throughout this book, the disability rights movement, steeped in whiteness, is in no way engaged in collective liberation as part of its work for change.

Let me explain with another story about my first encounters with the white disability rights community's celebrations. In June 2010 the community came together to celebrate the eleventh anniversary of the *Olmstead* case. This is how they refer to this landmark Supreme Court case. They erase the legacy of the Black disabled woman who was the lead plaintiff on this historic civil rights court ruling. At the time of writing this section Lois Curtis has just passed away from pancreatic cancer. She died in poverty and there is a GoFundMe campaign to ensure that she has a beautiful homegoing ceremony.

On June 22, 1999, the US Supreme Court held in *Olmstead v. Lois Curtis* that unjustified segregation of persons with disabilities constitutes discrimination in violation of Title II of the Americans with Disabilities Act. Basically, the institutionalization of disabled people is against their civil rights. The white disability rights community has decided to refer to this case as the *Olmstead* case, not only erasing Lois Curtis but uplifting Tommy Olmstead, who was a white man and commissioner of the Georgia Department of Human Resources. The white man who wanted to keep disabled people locked up in institutions. They would rather uplift and remember this white man than honor the plaintiff, Lois Curtis, a Black disabled woman.

It is rare that you hear people discuss a SCOTUS case in terms of one side; usually people refer to them in full case: *Brown v. Board of Education, Plessy v. Ferguson,* etc. But this is not a practice in the white disability rights community; they continuously write, discuss, and celebrate this case, even today, as "the *Olmstead* case," which is beyond disrespectful and more proof of their erasure of BIPOC disabled people's contributions to the fight for disability freedoms.

———

In 2010, as a TASH employee, I went to the celebration of SCOTUS's *Olmstead v. Lois Curtis* case and learned about two racist and patronizing comparisons made by members of the white disability rights community. One was about a prominent woman in the movement and the other was about the historic SCOTUS case.

This was the first time I was introduced to Yoshiko Dart. This amazing Japanese American woman was kind, and her smile was so welcoming. It was an honor to meet another person I had read about in Joe Shapiro's book. I was also excited to finally encounter a respected woman of color in this community. We immediately become steadfast friends and kindred spirits who remain sisters to this day. We share the same birthday!

It was the way in which a prominent white male advocate who is indecorously "revered" in the movement introduced Yoshiko to me that shook my inner Black woman core. He said, "Dara, have you met Yoshiko Dart? She is the Rosa Parks of the disability rights movement!" I was stunned, literally taken aback by his loud and proud statement. My mouth hung open for a few seconds. But I of course did not want to insult this amazing shero standing in front of me. Many in the room nodded in agreement and said, "Oh yes, she was there through it all," and some repeated, "Our Rosa Parks."

To this day I believe Yoshiko understood that comparing her to the revered Mrs. Rosa Parks was not flattering. She did not accept that title and she never has permitted it to be used in her introductions or recognitions at events. Yet others in the community have no problem with using this comparison, as if it is a compliment to be bestowed upon their iconic mother of the white disability rights movement.

Rosa Parks was an activist and thought leader who made a significant mark as a lead organizer in the civil rights movement. Contrary to what many believe, she did not just get up one morning and say, "I am going to refuse to give up my seat on that bus." She was arrested and spent her life fighting for the civil rights of Black people.

I completely and lovingly respect Yoshiko Dart and her many contributions to the disability rights movement. But there are other ways to honor her achievements that don't involve comparisons to Rosa Parks. The many books, articles, and writings done about Yoshiko Dart's contributions are condescending, representing her as the woman who assisted her husband, Justin Dart, in the imperative work of advancing the ADA into law. Justin Dart is the man who appears in most pictures sitting in his wheelchair with a cowboy hat on the White House lawn next to President Bush at the historic signing ceremony of the ADA. Together they went to all fifty states to discuss and advocate for the necessity of the passage of this historic civil right. The history written does not portray her in the significant and reverent way in which her story should be conveyed to the world. Yoshiko Dart was not only in the room; she was a true partner in the work and she continues to be a strong force and changemaker to this day!

After I was introduced to Yoshiko, the event started, and we all took to our seats. I was sitting there looking at the room full of mostly white people. There was serious irony in this, and I could not stop wondering if the organizers and attendees in the room found this as a contradiction of the celebration. In this US Supreme Court case we were there to celebrate, one of the co-plaintiffs, Lois Curtis, was a disabled Black woman. In all of the conversations that day about this historic case, and there were many, not once did these advocates or lawyers disclose this fact as a piece of important information for the case. This remains the modus operandi today in the conversations and discussions of this historic case.

I suspect this is because over all these years of being in spaces with all white people providing analysis, Lois's race never emerged as central to the case. This lack of desire to consider her race as a factor of the case remains today, because the field of experts continues to be dominated by white disability rights lawyers analyzing this case. There is angry pushback from white disability rights advocates when they are called out on the erasure of a disabled Black woman in this case. Many reply with, "She was not the only plaintiff on the case," or, "It's too long to write out the entire case."

In fact, Lois Curtis was the lead plaintiff on the case, which is the standard for citing court cases. The pushback on the length is yet another white excuse. This complaint is from a bunch of lawyers and policymakers who do not know brevity in writing or speaking.

At this celebration, speaker after speaker described the *Olmstead* case in the context of another racist, anti-Black, and patronizing comparison. They continuously compared this case to the *Brown v. Board of Education* Supreme Court case of 1954. "The Olmstead case is 'our' *Brown v. Board of Education* in the disability community." I was sitting in my chair calmly listening to these speeches, but on the inside I was fuming. How could these people actually use such a comparison? These cases and the decisions in them are completely different.

In *Olmstead v. Lois Curtis*, the court says that "unjustified segregation of persons with disabilities constitutes discrimination in violation of Title II of the Americans with Disabilities Act."[4] The decision in *Brown v. Board of Education* overturned the *Plessy v. Ferguson* decision of 1896, which legitimized the doctrine of "separate but equal." On May 17, 1954, the Supreme Court overturned *Plessy v. Ferguson* with a 9–0 decision that said "separate educational facilities are inherently unequal." This powerful landmark decision also legally recognized that "separate but equal" was in fact a violation of the Equal Protection Clause of the Fourteenth Amendment of the US Constitution.

My contempt for the disability rights community deepened that day in June 2010 as I sat listening to presenters comparing the *Olmstead v. Lois Curtis* case to *Brown v.*

Board of Education. I was the only Black person in the room working for one of those organizations and still fairly new to the disability rights community, so it was one of the few times I remained silent.

It was my duty to do some research and gather information before releasing my contempt and anger. But as the years went on, I was exposed to even more racist, anti-Black, and patronizing comparisons used by the white disability rights community. It made me be vocal in every situation, so much so that it led to the contempt and harm that I endured from this community. I wear those scars proudly.

———

Another racist and patronizing comparison done in the disability rights community is around "the Capitol Crawl." This is the momentous disability rights action done on March 12, 1990, on the steps of the US Capitol. In a move to get the ADA passed in the House of Representatives that year, advocates took to the stairs of the inaccessible US Capitol. Those with mobility disabilities could not enter the building through this entrance. This was glaring proof of the oppression of an entire community. They were people living in the US who could not enter the very building that stood for their freedom.

Over a thousand advocates from over thirty states came to the US Capitol, and after the speeches about why the ADA should be passed immediately, at least sixty people got out of their wheelchairs and began to crawl their way up the eighty-three steps of this historic legislative building. As they crawled, they chanted and demanded that Congress "Pass the ADA NOW!"

That is some amazing shit, right! I mean, that was effective in-your-face activism. Yet some in the community will compare this historic event to what the civil rights community did in Selma 1965. Yes, you are reading this right.

The first time I heard this, it came out of the mouth of yet another older white male who is wrongly "revered" in the disability rights community. He used it in many of his speeches and outreach to young disability rights activists. Unfortunately, like the other racist and patronizing comparisons discussed earlier, he was not the only one in the community who used this as an introduction and education into the disability rights movement. It was yet another example of the "direct with great force" power structure used to engage with the multi-marginalized. I was yet again taken aback and offended by this comparison.

The "Capitol Crawl" was done on the steps of the US Capitol and considered a peaceful direct action by all involved. There were no arrests and no reports of provoked or intentional harm. In Selma, there were a vast number of protests that lasted months, although many only learn about "Bloody Sunday." I am not being presumptuous to say that "Bloody Sunday" is the event referred to by disability rights community when they invoke this offensive comparison. Because I asked, "When you refer to Selma, what do you mean?" The reply was indignant and said with annoyance, "Bloody Sunday, of course!"

On March 7, 1965, a group of nonviolent civil rights activists attempted to cross the Edmund Pettus Bridge in the first march organized to fight voter suppression in the South. This was the first in a series of three-part protests set to display defiance to the repressive suppression of the Black vote. Those protests were organized and planned by James Bevel, who at the time was the Southern Christian Leadership Conference's director of direct action. Bevel wanted to use the anger and outrage of the Black community in Alabama to do something peaceful to explain the plight of his people. There was outrage in that community because in February 1965, civil rights activist and deacon Jimmie Lee Jackson was shot and killed by James Bonard Fowler, an Alabama state trooper.

What happened on the Edmund Pettus Bridge in Selma is known around the world as "Bloody Sunday." The peaceful demonstrators that day included the late iconic civil rights activist John Lewis, former Democratic congressman from Georgia. They were met on the bridge by Alabama state troopers and county posse men. This group of white, non-disabled men were mobilized by law enforcement and given special powers by the racist white governor of Alabama to suppress lawlessness and defend the county.[5]

This legally sanctioned mob warned the peaceful activists not to cross the county line. When these brave souls decided to continue forward with their nonviolent demonstration for the right to vote in this country, they were attacked with billy clubs to the head and body and had tear gas thrown in their faces. Some of these peaceful marchers were beaten unconsciousness. Luckily no one died that day.

The late great John Lewis and those peaceful demonstrators did this in hope of getting Congress to pass the Voting Rights Act of 1965, which was done in August of that year. I remain contemptuous when I hear the disability rights movement continue to compare the "Capitol Crawl" to Selma's "Bloody Sunday."

The final racist, anti-Black, and patronizing disability rights comparison that I will discuss is comparing escaping from a nursing home to the beloved and revered Harriet Tubman's Underground Railroad. It is through tears of anger that I recount this horrific act of misogynoir, which is rampant in the disability rights community. This was written in the 2008 article "Escaping the Nursing Home" for *New Mobility* magazine. There is even a section of the article titled "The Heroes of the Underground Railroad," which refers to those white people working in and around centers for independent living who get disabled people out of nursing homes.

The trauma of writing why this is offensive remains with me each day, because even today I am still pushing back on this horrific comparison. The fact that a bunch of white disability rights advocates think that there are similarities and overlapping experiences with their plight and the Underground Railroad is beyond appalling.

It is through clenched teeth and seething anger that I explain to these racist people that first and foremost, they cannot under any circumstances evoke, conjure, or discuss Harriet Tubman. Black women will not tolerate any disrespect to this woman's heritage. The Underground Railroad was used to get enslaved Black people in the United States to free states and Canada though treacherous routes, a network of trusted safe houses. It was created and implemented by the brilliant Harriet Tubman, who put her life and the lives of her people in danger every time she engaged in the work of abolitionism. You white racist disabled people do not get to compare your work of getting disabled people out of institutions where they were not enslaved to the historic life-changing work of Harriet Tubman. And most of the work of getting disabled people out of institutions was and continues to be done by white people not engaged in abolitionism, a sacred Black historical experience.

———

The disrespect of the white disability rights community happens through more than racist comparisons. The practice of hosting and promoting conversations and discussions about BIPOC experiences without those people being involved in the planning of or even being a part of the panel is another consistent part of the white supremacy work of the disability rights community. This disrespectful and harmful practice remains part of their outreach and work today and through the COVID-19 pandemic. Although many disabled BIPOC have informed white disability rights organizations of their outrage about this, these white-only panels and conversations about BIPOC issues remain at the forefront of most conferences, events, conversations, etc. The indignant white disability rights community does not find a need to change. This harmful injustice is a catalyst for the creation of disability justice.

In 2016 and 2018, two national disability rights organizations held their annual conference in the District, Maryland, and Virginia (DMV) area. This is typical of these organizations because they either want to get congressional members or staff, as well as the administration's staff, to come to and speak at their events. They have even been able to get sitting presidents to speak at their conferences. It is sad to say that President Obama and #45 are the recent sitting presidents who did not attend one disability organization's event and speak to their members while they were in the Oval Office. Many tried to get President Obama and Mrs. Obama to participate in multiple events over the eight years they were in the White House but to no avail.

At their annual conferences, these two national disability rights organizations decided to have panel discussions on some racial issues of serious concern to many BIPOC communities. They had, as they described, expert panelists speak on law enforcement and implicit bias at one, and at the other there was a training on the juvenile justice system and how implicit bias "plays a role" in the mass incarceration of millions of Black and Brown youth in our country. This sounds amazing and this was a direct response to the White House calling on organizations and advocates to have serious conversations with their members about these realities.

This was after the horrific killing of Trayvon Martin using the "stand your ground" law in Florida, the murder of Mike Brown by law enforcement in Ferguson, Missouri, and the launch of President Obama's My Brother's Keeper program. The groups were, as usual, trying to adhere to a request by the White House with no genuine desire to be involved in or create change in Black young men's lives. No work was done, because none of their organizations have ever done anything just for the Black community. They attended the events, so they could put that on their resume and boost their careers. The disability rights advocates who attended these events also were following the White House's lead by dominating this conversation with male cisgender voices and stories and trying to make themselves seem relevant to the conversation.

This all sounds good. Most annual conference themes are chosen to address current event concerns. But in this case one of the national disability rights organizations held a panel discussion on law enforcement killing people with disabilities with all white panelists. The panel was organized and planned by a completely white committee. It was titled "Finding Common Ground: Efforts to Promote Training and Advance Justice Between Law Enforcement and the Disability Community." It was on law enforcement and implicit bias, and the panel was completely made up of white people, although the title included the words "the Disability Community."

They discussed the only case that this community equates to the murdering of disabled people by the police. It is the case that hit them at their core and occurred in Maryland. It was the senseless killing of a young white male with a developmental disability by a Maryland law enforcement officer. I am not negating his horrible death; what I am doing by not even mentioning his name is putting forth the fact that there were a number of young Black and Brown people with developmental disabilities killed by law enforcement in Maryland prior to this young man's murder. Those parents and families never get discussed or put on panels to talk about their plight and fight for justice or the loss of their loved one. Yet again the disability rights community in the DMV participated in the erasure of an entire community's suffering.

The second panel was a training, held in 2018, about implicit bias in the juvenile justice system. It was planned and organized as well as facilitated by white women. The training discussed how implicit bias "plays a role" in the mass incarceration of millions of Black and Brown youth. They also discussed how many of these youth have disabilities and this manifests in their longer punishments and horrific treatments in the system. All of this is true, but the panel presented this with the message that implicit bias "plays a role" in mass incarceration, negating the thirty-plus years of evidence-based research on incarceration. It has been proven that implicit bias, racism, and white supremacy are the foundation of all our punitive systems. They don't "play a role."

Yes, this happened in 2016 and 2018 at national disability rights organizations' conferences in the DMV area. The organizers of these panels spent weeks if not months planning these important conversations. Yet none of them recognized the fact that a discussion on race and implicit bias was going to be done on a national level without BIPOC disabled voices on the panel.

I am a skeptic of the concept of implicit bias in general and in no way believe that the disability rights community in the DMV falls into this category of having implicit bias. According to the National Institutes of Health, implicit bias is "the thoughts that people have when they are unaware or they are mistaken about their nature. This is because when there are attitudes towards BIPOC people or associated stereotypes it is without the person's conscious knowledge."[6] I have been around this community intimately and professionally for over a decade, enough time to know that any actions it engages in around race are done intentionally, "direct with great force." They continue to intentionally host all-white panels on subject matters about BIPOC communities, as was proven during the COVID-19 pandemic with multiple panel discussions on the effects on the disabled community—the white disabled community. There is nothing implicit about their bias.

———

Why would a community do this?

It took me some time and numerous thoughtful conversations with many people in the disability rights community, much later in my career, to recognize why this community so eagerly emphasizes these racist and patronizing comparisons. They not only do this, but they also don't acknowledge the covert cynicism and racism of these associations. Or as many in the multi-marginalized disability communities believe, this majority purposely chooses to ignore these tendencies, using "direct with great force" power to silence the outrage. In fact, these comparisons remain part of the conversation at the writing of this book.

In 2018 comedian Tom Segura on his Netflix special titled *Disgraceful* made serious and derogatory comments about people with multiple types of disabilities as part of his show. The disability rights community, led by a prominent disability rights organization that works closely with those who have developmental disabilities, Down syndrome more specifically, created a petition, wrote letters to Netflix, wrote op-eds, and reached out to the press about their outrage over this comedian. There was a serious outcry, and numerous emails were sent out to many advocates across the country about how to shut this comedian down and end his show on Netflix. Several disability rights organizations joined in on this work with outreach to their membership and networks to get involved.

Then, a few weeks later, a known racist Republican congressman, Jason Lewis of Minnesota, compared the ADA to Jim Crow.[7] When this congressman from Minnesota made these comments there was complete silence from the disability rights community. Rep. Jason Lewis had a history of making racist and misogynistic remarks on his talk show, which he hosted prior to entering the legislative profession and working for the people. His repertoire included stating that "Black voters have an entitlement mentality" and "Young single women who voted based on contraceptive rights have no cognitive functions whatsoever."[8] He was quoted in multiple media outlets stating these things.

A member of the US House of Representatives made these racist comments about the ADA, and this was never addressed by any disability rights organization in the larger movement of DC. None of them sent a letter to this man asking him to apologize to the community, nothing was said to the media through op-eds or interviews to those same reporters who covered the controversy of Segura's remarks. Nothing was discussed about how insulting Lewis's comparison was to the millions of BIPOC with disabilities, specifically Black people. There was no outcry against Representative Lewis, a known racist with a history of being discriminatory toward most communities, to either be sanctioned or pushed out of his highly respected post in the US Congress. Why, you ask?

Let me go back to the comedian. I have my own thoughts on the work of comedians, as I am a staunch advocate for the First Amendment. Insults and inappropriateness are part of being a comedian. They push the envelope and cause people to think and be uncomfortable. The disability rights community has completely ignored the many comedians who are offensive to BIPOC, LGBTQIA+, Muslims—the list goes on and on for years. This is because the white disability rights community treats these communities as if they are not part of their full disability rights community. United States congressional members have a higher standard and are not only expected but legally obligated to work on behalf of all of their constituents.

I am not supporting or negating the effectiveness of comedians. I am acknowledging my frustration about the purposeful reaction of a community that consistently and resolutely selects the white voice as important in their work and continuously erases, suppresses, and insults all other voices, because this disabled white community refuses to acknowledge that even with their disability, they have white privilege and are part of the white supremacy of this country. This constant fight with aggressive, racist denialists contributes to my emotional trauma and that of many others who try to work collectively with this community, and many of us have ceased to try anymore.

———

Another example of erasure and covert disenfranchisement on the political side of this work highlights my thoughts about how members of the white disability rights community put protecting their career trajectory at the forefront of their work. They also present themselves and completely deny their privilege or the fact that they use this as a tool to be destructive of any progress that multi-marginalized communities put forth.

It is quite obvious that the leadership and most of the disability rights community in DC are heavily if not completely made up of Democrats. Those in power are not just registered Democrats; they are powerful donating proud members of the Democratic National Committee (DNC). There is a group of powerful Republican disabled advocates, but they are less active in the Republican National Committee (RNC). The disabled DNC crew is so powerful, and after years of developing this power, its members were finally able to get disability issues mentioned by candidates and onto the platform as a serious issue and concern for the 2016 election season. This group of DNC powerhouses was also able to create a disability rights group called the Disability Council within the DNC. But please take note and remember this did not occur until after the June 22, 2017, ADAPT takeover in Senator Mitch McConnell's office in the fight to save the Affordable Care Act (ACA). (Things that make you say, Umm.) This was the catalyst for the disability political power in DC being revamped.

This powerful political group has been able to host fundraisers and events for and with DNC leadership. In all of their work they have been able to influence the leadership to make some decisions about hiring people with disabilities and create space for actually training and encouraging disabled people to run for office. All of these things are quite amazing, considering both of these political parties have serious issues with multi-marginalized communities being in positions of leadership. They only need and work with our communities when they count the votes.

In my example above, the disability rights community went into full protection mode over a comedian's insulting jokes about those with developmental disabilities. The members of this Disability Council of the DNC, which garnered great power and yields it so well they gained employment and the space to push candidates with disabilities in the DNC, chose to purposefully remain silent during the 2019 blackface event regarding Virginia Democratic governor Ralph Northam. Every DNC group you can think of wrote a letter and publicly denounced Northam, as well as demanding that he immediately leave his position as governor. Who did not do this? The DNC Disability Council, which did nothing publicly or internally. (I know this because, although I am not a member of this council, I am on their email listserv—knowledge is power.)

There is no letter, no statement, or any document on record that expresses their disgust at a Democratic governor's horrific participation in racist acts. Many of us sat and waited "in the cut," as they say, to watch how this unfolded. True to form, this disability community ignores a harmful, hateful event that is offensive to Black people, people who are part of their movement, people who are part of their voting block. And they continue to question why the disabled BIPOC community is so angry with them.

There is a caste system that exists in the disability rights community, one where white cisgender disabled people are the privileged higher caste and all others are the lower caste. It is a system that has roots in and permeates from other cultures, such as the caste system of oppression around Dalit apartheid.

In my activism I am blessed to work with several amazing advocates, policymakers, lawyers, and thought leaders. One of these people is the "Dalit diva," Thenmozhi Soundararajan, author of the amazing book *The Trauma of Caste: A Dalit Feminist Meditation on Survivorship, Healing, and Abolition.* She is a phenomenal woman who has dedicated her life to ending the caste apartheid system in this world. I also am a life learner and attend many seminars, training sessions, and all other learning spaces. Thenmozhi is also the executive director of Equality Labs, and she has a fabulous team. She uses art and healing as the center of her outreach and conversation around what the caste system is and its appalling effects on the world.

Equality Labs designed and conducted the first ever survey on the caste system in the United States. The title of their report is *Caste in the United States: A Survey of Caste Among South Asian Americans.* If you have not read it, please do today and join us in our work to dismantle the caste apartheid system.

What is caste? Caste determines access to opportunities for advancement as well as to ownership of resources, i.e., arable land, clean water, education, and employment. As I stated, Thenmozhi is the Dalit diva. Dalits are caste communities that were forced by caste apartheid into slave and agricultural labor and undignified sanitation work like manual scavenging. Branded untouchable for jobs considered spiritually polluting, they struggle against extreme violence and discrimination.

Caste apartheid is a structure of oppression that affects over one billion people across the world. It is a system of religiously codified exclusion that was established in Hindu scripture. At birth, every child inherits his or her ancestor's caste, which determines social status and assigns "spiritual purity."[9]

This idea that your life's path is determined at birth is at the core of the disability rights fight, especially for those born with a disability. They continue to fight for the right to live the independent life they set for themselves with their own dreams and desires. There are laws and Supreme Court cases that provide them with the rights to do this, and yet society has not accepted these terms for their lives.

In my work on social justice and working around numerous multi-marginalized communities, I observe that this caste system from India and perpetuated by the Hindu faith is present in almost all of these groups. In the disability community a caste system also exists, as I have been discussing. But here is where the rubber meets the road. There is little to no difference between our oppressive society and the caste system, nor is there any difference in how the majority in the caste system and in our system continue to oppress.

In the disability rights community, the white disabled falsely do not think of themselves as part of the majority or the privileged or higher caste. But they very much are. They are adamant that their disability precludes them from being part of a higher caste. The privileged, which let me be clear does include white disabled people, will sit in denial, hurl insults, and tell the oppressed that we have misinterpreted, don't really understand, or are overly sensitive. None of these things will create genuine change in this atrocious caste disability system and is part of the reason multi-marginalized communities are mistreated horribly in the disability rights movement.

In the disability rights community, comparing the plight of white disabled people as equal to or even sometimes more important than others' removes them from the work of collective liberation. In fact, it makes them part of the system of oppression and a long history of white supremacy pitting marginalized people against one another. This type of community manipulation has its history in this country as far back as slavery and its origins with white wealthy landowning men. White slave masters used hierarchy based on the shade of skin color to set forth and distinguish the "house niggas" from the "field niggas." This forced antagonism remains a destructive force in the Black community for many to this day, manifesting in the hatred of having dark skin.

Michelle Alexander discusses in her dynamic book *The New Jim Crow* how the wealthy white men went to the poor white men and used comparisons of how freed slaves would be competition for them in their plight to thrive. It was how the white male landowner minority in this country was able to quash the freeing of the enslaved. Alexander describes this in the introductory chapter of her poignant book to set the tone and lay the foundation for the knowledge she spouts upon you about race and this country's farcical system of justice.

She discusses the uprising of a collaborative effort by poor whites and Black slaves in Jamestown, Virginia, led by Nathaniel Bacon. Bacon's Rebellion was an attempt to overturn the power structure, which was dominated by wealthy white landowners who were in the minority. In his attempt to overthrow Jamestown leadership, Bacon was able to bring together bond workers or indentured slaves and the enslaved, who fought against the elite white landowners or planters.

Bacon's Rebellion was lost due to multiple factors, but its destruction left an opening for the elite white male landowners to create systems of oppression and racist conflict that have remained part of the United States fabric of existence until this day. In this context of pitting oppressed communities against each other, the white male planters dismantled their use of indentured white servants and turned to using the enslaved from Africa. "Deliberately and strategically, the planter class extended special privileges to poor whites in an effort to drive a wedge between them and Black slaves."[10] They removed any future alliances between these two groups, and the poor whites fell into societal place within this caste system of oppression on Black and Indigenous people, all non-white male landowners.

In the early years of the 1900s' civil rights movement in this country, white Christian men put a wedge between the Jewish and Black communities using some of these same tactics. They told Jews that they had a better living and could be happy in their state of marginalization as it was nothing compared to the Black and Brown peoples. At the same time, they encouraged Jewish people to participate in disenfranchisement of the Black and Brown community of this country. That worked well because these tensions remain in our communities. This is especially true with those of us who are steadfast in support of our Palestinian family in their fight to end oppression from the Jewish state.

There remains tension between Black feminists and anger regarding much of the white feminist movement, a movement that left behind the plight of all other women in this country once they got much of what they demanded. This is the same group that refuses to discuss the large white female voting block for the past election seasons where Republican despots have won their positions of leadership because many of them voted for these people. There is a consistent denial by white feminists to discuss the white women voter numbers—54 percent in 2016 and 57 percent in 2020 for #45 and then in 2022, the 73 percent who voted for Governor Kemp in Georgia. This is the majority displacing the anger and not being responsible for the problems they have caused yet again.

———

In the early years of my disability work, it was my intent as the only BIPOC in a policy position in the DC disability rights community to find out why this happened and to call this out in the hope of change. My two cohorts of color who I met in 2010 left this work. One departed in 2012 and the other left in 2013. This is not uncommon in disability rights policy work. On the rare occasion that they hired BIPOC policy staff, they usually only lasted twelve to eighteen months. I am probably the BIPOC policy staffer who lasted the longest in this community: ten consecutive years.

I set forth to learn where such behavior originated. I gathered this information from reading a number of books and having numerous conversations on the history of the disability rights movement. Those talks were with lots of people both in the book *No Pity* and others not in the book but from around the country who I met and worked with over the decade.

The above reviews of how the majority overtly engages in pitting communities against one another are just some of the examples of how many disability rights advocates have learned to function in social justice and civil rights movements in this country. They observed, learned from, and unfortunately took away all the bad traits of these movements.

What I have determined is that many in the disability rights community honestly do not perceive anything wrong with how they present their history to the world. They decisively have not worked with other disenfranchised communities for over twenty years. In 2019, at a disability symposium event, a white woman admitted this in a Q&A discussion. She spoke about the fact that these problems have been around for years and gone unaddressed by an entire community and how until this is discussed nothing will change. In all that time, the disability rights community eagerly used these racist, anti-Black, and patronizing comparisons without inquiring with other communities to find out if it was disrespectful or if they should be used.

These are insulting, discriminatory, oppressive, and racist behaviors, to think and say that these precious and historic fights for Black liberation are similar to or have overlapping tendencies with white disabled history. Yet they push back in anger and proudly yell that they do not view things that way. For over a decade and even now I have continued to tell them that because one feels they are doing nothing wrong is not an excuse nor is it correct. The offender does not get to make that decision. And I am hated by many in the white disability rights community for my outspoken, up-front, and honest analysis of their horrible movement.

They are not clueless; they are the very essence of denial of their white privilege. This is proven because they get
self-satisfaction that is accompanied by smugness and glee
when they compare Yoshiko Dart (much respect) to Rosa
Parks, the *Olmstead v. Lois Curtis* SCOTUS case to *Brown v.
Board of Education*, the "Capitol Crawl" to Selma ("Bloody
Sunday"), and the deinstitutionalization of disabled people
to the precious honor of the Underground Railroad.

Did they just not know who to go to for these answers?

Not at all, for as this community consistently puts forth,
they got their model for fighting the ADA from the civil
rights movement, yet they never honor the heroes of that
movement. Many of their leaders had long and lasting relationships with a number of civil rights icons. A number of
these disability rights organizations have been and remain
individual members of the Leadership Conference on Civil
and Human Rights. There are several BIPOC leaders and
organizations they could form collaborations with and learn
from, but they have purposefully chosen not to engage in
this type of work.

Two of these groups have served on the board of the
Leadership Conference, for well over twenty years. But this
is more window dressing. One of these groups is completely
inactive in the work, as they don't attend any of the working group meetings, do any policy work like congressional
visits, or write letters to Congress. They do no meaningful
advocacy outreach or policy work yet serve on the nation's
leading civil and human rights coalition's board as "the
voice" of disability issues.

These organizations are not involved in the Leadership
Conference with the intentional or strategic social justice
plan to genuinely engage other communities. They do this so

that it looks good on their resumes used for funding those fake DEI programs and to appear as good collaborators in dismantling oppression for those philanthropic funds.

They had access to a number of groups and leaders who could advise them on race relations and outreach. They purposefully chose not to use these resources. Instead they intentionally dismiss the outcry of disabled BIPOC and multi-marginalized communities by yielding "direct with great force" power. It is yet another racist conundrum that I, as the only Black person in these DC rooms working on multiple policy issues, have tried unsuccessfully to dismantle.

DISABILITY IN THE BELTWAY

I n 2017, the entire "progressive movement" decided that they would come together and protect one of the most valued laws created during the Obama administration: the Affordable Care Act (ACA), or what was inevitably referred to by the right wing as "Obamacare." In the disability rights movement here in DC, the leaders decided that they would join in this collaborative effort to protect the ACA at all costs. It was one of the few times they branched out and worked with other civil and human rights groups.

The Consortium for Citizens with Disabilities (CCD) was the leading disability rights organization on this campaign. But of course they could not do this without superiority or elitism, for that is how they function. They decided that two of their task forces, health and long-term services and supports (LTSS), would lead the disability outreach. They also decided that they would "allow" others from around the country to participate in this fight. This resistance could not be done without help, input, and disruption from outside the DC Beltway. It was a known fact that CCD used them as a pawn in the game. They needed the large crowds at their rallies. They had no genuine meaningful outreach for creating collaborative relationships. As soon as the fight to save the ACA was over, they cut all ties with these groups.

Those groups are not located in DC and therefore cannot be members of CCD.

In this work, CCD had no chance of blocking others' involvement as this was a fight for their lives, and so working with others outside the DC Beltway was not a decision that they came to easily. But what they did was bully their way to the lead and created a condescending process to "include" others in the work. It was done in their true form as they used their privilege to run this collaboration. This started with segregating the groups and creating distinction between these groups. They called the professional policy staff group by the TF name and in a condensing way called the others the grassroots group. There were two different listservs, and the grassroots members were not allowed or welcomed to be a part of the professional policy TF. All this was done as if the grassroots people were not on the same educational or experience level as the professionals; yet they were all working to save the same law that assisted all people.

I was not an active participant in this work through this TF, as I had my own fight to lead where I used collaborative and inclusive methods for fighting for a cause. That cause was an all-out attack on the ADA with a horrible bipartisan-supported bill: the ADA Education and Reform Act (H.R. 620) in the 115th Congress. In my work I reached out to multiple coalitions and organizations to try to get them to work as one unit. This coalition to save the ADA worked collaboratively as one group and obtained various letters of opposition that were signed by local, state, and national organizations. In fact, one letter of opposition to H.R. 620 garnered signatures from more than two hundred organizations. This is how I work collectively to create change, and it's a model I use in almost all of my policy and activism work. It is one of the reasons I am seen as an interference to the work of CCD, which works so tirelessly to block out this type of collaborative policy work.

I was actively involved in the fight to save the ACA through my membership in two on-the-ground organizations but not through my professional work. In the first few days of the resistance, emails went out and a new group within the larger group was formed. This is not unusual as many coalitions create working groups to address immediate issues. What was different about this new working group was its name, its mission, who led this group, and how the group was discussed by CCD. It was the decision of CCD leadership to create a separate group of grassroots advocates who would be guided and led by them to do the right things in this fight against the despot in the White House and a Republican-led Congress set to dismantle this imperative law.

CCD chose to set up the two different groups as a way to block the use of disruption and direct-action strategies for accomplishing policy change. This process did not work because on June 22, 2017 (the anniversary of *Olmstead v. Lois Curtis*), the group ADAPT, known for direct action, took over Leader Mitch McConnell's office. Those images were seen and respected by millions around the world.

This was just one example of how CCD and many other DC Beltway organizations treat grassroots activists. It is why I hate the term so much. As I tell many in my trainings, conversations, and speeches, I don't use the term "grassroots" because the DC Beltway treats them as lesser than. This condescending way of "explaining" how policy is done in DC to those who are closest to the problem is one of the huge barriers to dismantling these systems of oppression and racism. These covert, rigged, and often deliberative actions done by the disability rights community and specifically DC Beltway policy groups actually cause harm. It is those people who are closest to the problem who have the solutions. Until this is recognized and respected by elite DC Beltway organizations like CCD, there will be no new world order.

Creating a separate working group and treating them as if they are not equal to the DC Beltway group is where all things went wrong after the fight to save the ACA for the disability rights community. CCD has criteria and rules for organizations to join. This is not unusual as many coalitions have membership standards. But CCD has created a system that specifically blocks out groups. It is how they create the closed environment for which they want to do policy work.

The criterion for membership in CCD is that any member of this group must have a DC presence or office, and they do not allow volunteers to be a part of their policy TFs. Now, this is the unusual part for a DC coalition group and was implemented only in the past few years. Although I am using this community as an example, let me say that this kind of elitism, supremacy, paternalism, and all disrespectful adjectives you can think of occur in all issue areas of policy work in DC and around the country.

But since we had a despot in the White House and a not-so-friendly US Congress, most coalitions embraced the rule of "all people on deck"! They took on the attitude that said if you have a talent and want to assist us in this fight to protect what we have, come and get to work. Oh, but not in the disability rights community and certainly not in CCD. They created rules that purposefully and intentionally blocked out the participation of others who do not fit into their DC elite environment and others who want to assist and be part of the fight, mainly volunteers.

How does this affect the work?

It is elitism and white privilege at its best because there is a system of never holding these people accountable for their actions, like racist patronizing comparisons and the erasure of Black leaders, as discussed earlier in this book. Those who push back and call out these things are ignored or, worse, made out to be "angry" and not people that they can work with to accomplish the goals. This type of working environment sets up a concrete structure where nothing is done to create systemic changes and those in control keep all the power. Isn't this the actual thing that social justice and civil rights groups are supposed to fight or better yet dismantle?

This affected my activism and participation eligibility in CCD because in January 2019, I went to work for the Center for Disability Rights in New York, which was a state entity, but hiring me, they expanded their outreach and became a national organization. I was their first staff member in DC. My position also elevated a Black woman to a position as a director of national policy. But in this new position, I would have to volunteer to be part of CCD as my new organization was not a member and denied membership.

I volunteered with CCD back in 2013 when I went to work for the DC government in the Office of Disability Rights (ODR) under Mayor Vince Grey. They had no problems with me volunteering my time and participating in the coalition when I worked for a "respectable" organization, as a position in the DC mayor's office is a prominent one.

I worked on multiple CCD TFs and on issues and policies during my time in ODR. I was on listservs and attended meetings on my own time. But when I went to work for a group that is not part of the DC Beltway and that was outside the boundaries of control and not respectable to them this caused a problem. My new organization applied for membership into CCD and was denied acceptance as a member supposedly because they had no DC presence—even though I was in DC working on national policy.

I offered to volunteer my time with CCD in this new role, as I had done before. The first thing I was told by the CCD chair, a nondisabled cisgender upper-middle-class white woman, was that I could no longer hold my leadership positions, which was as a cochair of any task force. I had been a cochair for over five years and for four task forces; one TF I revamped was the Emergency Management TF. I put it back together after four years of people saying they were going to get this done but with no results. I had no recourse to fight this outright racist process because CCD did not have a process for me to hold them accountable. I went to my fellow cochairs and let them know that I would be stepping down from my position immediately as instructed by the chair but had plans to remain as a member of the TFs.

One month into my new position, the chair of CCD sent out an email with a new rule and criteria for members of the coalition. Volunteers are not allowed to be a part of task forces. Now, I had been a member of CCD for ten years and seen volunteers come and go working in TFs with no problems. But when I became a volunteer in TFs, this chair decided that rule had to end. I was told that I could not attend any TF meetings or events. As I talked to many in CCD, they let me know that they thought this rule was wrong and they believed I was being targeted. But only a few actually said something about their concerns to the chair and they were quickly silenced.

This calculated racist process to block me out of CCD DC Beltway disability policy work only stopped me from working with one organization. So I went to my other co-alitions around DC that I have worked with for the years I have been doing social justice work in DC and they had no problems with me remaining as an active member. They also did not make me give up any of my leadership positions. In fact, I remain on steering committees and was elevated to cochair of the Transportation Equity Caucus.

It was only in the DC disability rights movement that these elitist, supremacist, and racist attitudes were put into action. In a time when we were fighting one of the worse despots in the White House, what coalitions who are doing civil rights/social justice work turn away volunteers to help in this fight? This is what the DC white disability rights co-alition does and with pride.

In review of the "make up" of CCD, let us remember, there are over one hundred organizations, only about seven are run by and for people with disabilities or are run by women, and there are few openly LGBTQIA+ people on policy staffs. There are no national disability rights organi-zations working on policy in DC or in CCD led by and for BIPOC or members of multi-marginalized disabled commu-nities. The majority of the policy people working in CCD in 2020 are middle class or wealthy, nondisabled, cisgender, educated, white women who have purposefully created a space that blocks out organizations from around the nation and anyone who wishes to volunteer. Those who are willing to volunteer their time to help protect civil rights of disabled people are not welcomed.

———

In "progressive movements" such as disability rights there is the belief that as disabled people they cannot possibly benefit from white privilege. This falsehood causes the whitewashing of the public policy agendas. What does that mean and look like?

First let me review the definitions of *white privilege* and *whitewashing* as discussed in the glossary section of this book. *White privilege* is the deeper comprehension of how critical race theory analyzes how racism and racialized societies affect the lives of white people. It denotes both obvious and less obvious passive advantages that white people may not recognize they have.

I am using the informal definition of *whitewashing*, which refers to "defeat (an opponent), keeping them from scoring" because the white disability rights movement does not want to see BIPOC disabled community win at much of anything. In the media, *whitewashing* refers to the tendency of media to be dominated by white actors, navigating their way through a story that will likely resonate most deeply with white audiences based on their experiences and worldviews.

In the disability rights movement when multi-marginalized communities and specifically Black people call out racism, discrimination, and injustices in the work, often the response given by white disability rights advocates is that they could not possibly benefit from white privilege because they are disabled. This did not amaze me the first time I heard it because I had lived through the actions and the advocacy campaigns well before these words were said.

The thought that white disabled people are immune to white privilege is something you recognize immediately upon reading about or working in disability rights. It is considered an obvious truth. Of course it is, because when the room is full of those people who think and work this way (white people) with no voice of difference (BIPOC and multi-marginalized people) the outcome is inevitably going to be this kind of prejudice and marginalization.

It is also because many in the disability rights movement (well, to be honest, the general white public) do not have an understanding of what exactly white privilege is or how it has affected the systems and structures of disenfranchisement and marginalization in this country, well, really, this world. This is no excuse for the behavior or the work, but it is a partial view into the psyche of those leading the disability rights community.

In the book *White Fragility*, by Robin DiAngelo, this is discussed as an assumption: "White people who experience another form of oppression cannot experience racial privilege."[1] She explains the logic as follows: "Highlighting my racial privilege invalidates the form of oppression that I experience (e.g., classism, sexism, heterosexism, ageism, ableism, transphobia)."

Most people look at white privilege as only relating to classism, which then reflects the advantages of white people in spaces where they have the freedom to move, buy, work, play, and speak freely. They have advantages in the areas of profession, education, home ownership, transportation, etc. This is how some poor white people and, in this case, disabled white people try to justify that they do not reap the benefits of white privilege because they have been barred from these privileges.

What most do not recognize is that white privilege has obvious advantages as mentioned above as well as passive or cultural advantages. These passive advantages remove white people from biases and prejudices and continue to perpetuate the basis of white privilege, which makes all others different or exceptional, and they see themselves as normal or as correct and all others are wrong. In the case of disability, as has been discussed throughout this book, disabled advocates and the movement for disability rights view white disabled people as "normal" and other multi-marginalized BIPOC, specifically Black disabled people, as something different or exceptional.

———

This attitude, along with the dominance of white people holding the power in the disability rights movement, has led to whitewashing in public policy and advocacy. What does this look like and how is this harmful to social equity work?

The work being done in CCD is distributed among those multiple task forces and dominated by cisgender nondisabled upper-middle-class white women. They have no lived experience and are not directly impacted by any of the issues they do policy agenda and outreach for.

These endeavors have been in existence for over forty years with little to no change or attempts to dismantle this oppressive system. In January 2020, a new advocacy year started and one of the cochairs of a TF proudly proclaimed that this would be their twenty-fifth year in this position. What makes matters worse is that they found nothing wrong with these facts, and they honestly believe they are doing nothing but great work for disabled people.

They have dominated the work being done in Congress, the administration, and throughout the country for over forty years. There is no process to decide which disability issues to advocate for. This group does not engage in survey systems or inquiries of the community. Some organizations come to the work with information from their membership, but in actuality the decisions are made by those who hold the power. They, not the community (disabled people), decide who will lead the work and what those issues will be every year.

This is not so different from other national social justice and civil rights coalitions in DC. There are a number of issue areas worked on in DC that are predominantly led by white people who have no real-life experience with or connection to these issues, but they are leading the policy changes. I see this in housing equity and ending homelessness, in transformative justice reform and dismantling the criminal justice system. It is always a bonding moment with advocates and activists of color who come to DC for meetings or events and witness this firsthand.

Many of them notice this back at home in their work, but it is a stirring experience when the reality sinks in that mostly cisgender, upper-middle-class white people are speaking for their community in these spaces of power here in DC. They also see it as an explanation as to why there are serious barriers to achieving the systems changes they not only desire but find absolutely necessary for creating a new world order.

But some of the coalitions around DC do use surveys and conversations with their members around the country to decide on the issues that will be worked. Not all but most decisions are done in this manner. Coalitions like the Transportation Equity Caucus and the Federal School Discipline and Climate Coalition. These groups also embrace, with respect, people on the front lines and in the community to be active members in the change. This is not possible for CCD, because their membership criteria intentionally create barriers and keep groups and communities not in the DC Beltway out.

The absence of BIPOC and multi-marginalized people, and specifically those who are Black and Brown and disabled, in the decision-making creates whitewashed policy work. In the area of education equity policy there is a lot of work being done on the education and inclusion of disabled students. There is also a lot of work being done on dismantling restraint and seclusion of disabled students. But you will not find CCD or its many members of the Education TF working on or prioritizing the school-to-prison pipeline, police-free schools, or ending corporal punishment. These are all policies that harm BIPOC disabled students at a higher rate than their white disabled counterparts.

In transportation, many of these groups work on accessibility of the system but do not in any way work on equity or criminalization of the system. In housing, CCD has a few groups that work on our AA, which is accessible and affordable housing. But they do not work on racism, equity, and justice in housing. In healthcare, they work on issues that do not include racial or justice equity in their policy agenda. They do not make dismantling forced institutionalization a priority in the policy agenda.

Their whitewashed policy agenda messages that the only reason to use healthcare LTSS is to stay home. What is missing from this message is that so many are not at home. The white people who created this message based it on their white privileged experience of actually being at home. This message of only needing LTSS for staying home is not inclusive of all, because it leaves out the thousands of disabled people stuck inside institutions. Research has proven that disabled BIPOC and in particular Black disabled are forced into institutions at a higher rate than other groups of disabled people. During the height of the COVID-19 pandemic, the highest numbers of deaths were in these horrible institutions, which disabled people have been fighting to get out of for decades.

In voting rights, they work on the accessibility of the voting process, but there is little to no work done on voter suppression, disenfranchisement, or disenchantment. These are voting rights issues for BIPOC and other multi-marginalized communities. The list continues in almost every issue area you find the disability rights community working. As long as you continue to have cisgender upper-middle-class white nondisabled people leading the policy agenda it will remain whitewashed and the systemic change that BIPOC disabled people seek will never be achieved.

This is part of the change that needs to happen not only in disability policy and advocacy work but in all "progressive" policy agendas. Those of us who continue to bring this conversation to the table are shunned, insulted, and cut out by those with the power.

———

It is for these and many of the other reasons listed throughout this book that I decided to take my knowledge, passion, and talent for creating change in disability issues and work outside the white disability rights movement community. My decision to move into working in other coalitions came easy, because I came from those groups. I was blessed to have an established relationship with coalitions led by some BIPOC and multi-marginalized communities who understood our plight and infused that in their policy work.

What I had to bring to the table was unique as there was no disability rights voice at those tables. I started to attend those meetings in multiple coalitions around the country, on criminal justice and juvenile justice reform, reproductive justice, housing, transportation, LGBTQIA+ issues, and many others that are not taken seriously by the disability rights community. These are also groups that few if any of the white disability rights groups are part of and so I could happily avoid running into or working with any of them. Not being in spaces with them gave me relief from the constant harm. This remains an emotional joy in my work today.

The work in those coalitions is about the issues and policy concerns of multi-marginalized communities. It is work that is dear to my heart and important to those I love. This is work that is not being done in disability rights; in fact, it is not only ignored by many but is also regarded as a hindrance to disability policy. When confronted by disabled BIPOC people about why disability rights will not include their life-or-death issues, many of the replies are: "I am so sick of hearing about race and all these other groups!" "Intersectionality is a divisive term!" "We are disabled or we are working in disability rights—we can't possibly be racist in our work!" These are the various quotes from multiple national white disability rights advocates heard over and over as explanations.

An example of this is the work being done around justice reform. According to Roy Walmsley of the International Centre for Prison Studies and editor of the *World Prison Population* newsletter, "More than 9.8 million people are held in penal institutions throughout the world. . . . Almost half of these are in the United States. . . . The United States has the highest prison population rate in the world."[2] Most of those people are Black and Brown and disabled. People with disabilities represent a disproportionate share of America's prison population. This is evidenced-based research that has been discussed in various reports, books, articles, and policy briefs. We have the facts, but are DC organizations actually working to right these wrongs?

In the past five years there has been some movement in the area of prison reform. Unfortunately, in December

2018, the First Step Act (FSA) passed into law. At the time I worked for National Disability Rights Network (NDRN), and we were one of the first to send a letter of opposition to Congress, at my urging as the senior policy analyst on this subject matter. This letter was sent mainly because the law does nothing to assist the disabled in the system but also because there was so much more wrong than there was right with the legislation now law.

In the many years that I have worked in disability policy in DC there has never been an interest in prison reform or justice reform in CCD. There are some organizations within the group that work on pieces of the justice system, and they work on this from a whitewashed policy view of victimization not criminalization. When this was an important issue for the Obama administration CCD advocates pretended to be interested in this issue as part of that career trajectory process to look good for the DNC machine, but they did not do this work intentionally with a desire to create systems change. CCD has no standing committees or TFs that focus on the work of justice reform. This is another form of the power structure blocking out the voices of the people; for if they surveyed the community, it is quite certain that BIPOC disabled and those multi-marginalized would place ending criminalization and mass incarceration as priorities for their communities.

When it came time to stand up and advocate against some harmful amendments within the FSA and try to get some good disability language placed into the legislation, there were no disability rights DC Beltway groups working on this issue, except the one I represented, NDRN. This is not an issue of concern for CCD members or their policy work.

There were a number of opposition letters sent to Congress on the FSA. This was supposed to be a sentencing

reform bill that addressed mandatory minimums and conditions in prisons. Yet we could not get language into the bill
that would save our young people's lives or end the horrific
practice of solitary confinement. The US Congress decided
to take action on sentencing but purposefully left out ending
Juvenile Life Without Parole (JLWOP) language. We could
not get language in this bill to protect our youth or end the
despicable practice of torture used in our prison systems.
These are just two of the multiple problems with this law.

It is an interesting and not commonly known fact that
there were six Black women leaders who sent those letters
of opposition on FSA to Congress. The courage of Black
women never disappoints me. The groups who were vocal
about their opposition to FSA were Black Lives Matter, Human Rights Watch (the DC office's ED was a Black woman),
JustLeadership USA, the National Council for Incarcerated
and Formerly Incarcerated Women and Girls (both of these
organizations at that time were led by Black women who are
formerly incarcerated), National Council of Churches (their
senior policy person was a Black woman), the Movement
for Black Lives, and NDRN, where I was a senior policy
analyst. It is an honor to work with these Black women and
the many activists around the world to end criminalization
and mass incarceration, one that I do not share with the
disability rights community in the DC Beltway working on
civil and human rights.

————

Dr. Martin Luther King Jr. said, "The ultimate measure of
a man is not where he stands in moments of comfort and
convenience, but where he stands at times of challenge and
controversy."[3] Profound words said by a man who created

change through peaceful demonstration and used disruption as a tool to create change in this country.

Why don't "progressive" organizations like the CCD follow the wise words of Dr. King? Why, instead, do DC Beltway disability rights organizations use their power to discourage the use of direct action in the fight for the cause? Why does the DC Beltway or "block way" community deliberately undermine disruption and protesting as a means of creating systemic change?

Because they are protecting their position of power, the funds their organizations generate, and, in particular, their careers. They need that proximity to Congress and the White House. They want those invitations to events and galas to keep coming, and it is a known fact that if you do not "go along to get along," that proximity will cease to exist. All the while, front-line people are fighting to protect lives and end oppression with urgency and "by any means necessary."

The disability rights DC Beltway groups engage in creating a distinct line between being the policy people who do things "the right way" and those who cause disruption and are doing things "the wrong way"! They are proud to tell congressional members, "We will never come into your office and cause disruption." Those groups rarely if ever do direct action or agitate congressional offices. They grip onto that proximity with a tight fist. That is their privilege and prerogative to function in safety. They are not directly impacted by these issues. As I have stated, they have no urgency in their work, so this strategy is par for the course.

The foulness in this part of their work is to take those assertions and place them upon BIPOC disabled people who are putting their lives on the line and agitating, disrupting, and creating change. This is how white nondisabled and some disabled leaders in the disability rights movement hold power through supremacist psychological work. They use the model where they are at the center of the work and not disabled people because, of course, the powerful "know what is best for this community."

I, like many others fighting the good fight, am an activist at the core of my being, and I completely believe that disruption in all its forms is the central reason change has been realized. It's the way further changes will be accomplished, especially in this racist country.

There is so much to unpack and analyze in this patronizing and racist strategy to keep the power and maintain the status quo held by CCD and many others around the country. As Robin DiAngelo says, "I believe that 'white progressives' cause the most daily damage to people of color."[4] Disability rights progressives, along with most white progressives, believe that the system is good and that we just need to "make adjustments." This is so far from the truth and one of the many reasons we need them to move out of leadership.

These are the same "progressive" organizations and people that will pepper their request for proposals for funding from philanthropy with words and phrases that allow them to present themselves as "woke" and creating change. They use these phrases and words to create a false narrative or to clean up some obvious heinous dysfunction within their work, such as having an entirely white professional staff in 2022 who is set to implement their equity plan, which includes all-white panel discussions on implicit bias. "We believe that racial equity is essential to our outreach in creating change" or "Intersectionality is a core value that we use in our programs." They also use "structural racism" and "systems change" as buzzwords in these requests for funds.

They continue to have groups that do not include or uplift those with lived experience of disability or directly impacted as part of the solution. This perpetuates that 1960s attitude that created the War on Poverty, a program led by wealthy white people set to create changes for those living in poverty based on solutions they felt were best for the community. The truth is many progressives don't believe in and are far from being any more aware of the problems with this racist system than some of their conservative right-wing counterparts, who receive funding to suppress and destroy these same white progressives' conscious (woke) selves.

In doing social justice work, one can't believe that the oppressive racist system in this country is good and only needs some "tweaks and adjustments" to create safe and just spaces for BIPOC and multi-marginalized communities. This is an oxymoron. This is the modus operandi for white disability rights organizations.

———

I describe this when giving speeches and use the analogy of playing chess. The first and most egregious mistake made is thinking that the king is the most powerful piece on the board and that is so far from the truth. If you play chess then you know it is the queen. The action of uplifting Black Queens is more than using the term as some social media hashtag. It is the evidence-based affirmation that Black women have always been the foundation of liberation.

The second mistake is playing chess as if it were checkers (lack of political knowledge). In chess you must see the entire board, strategize, and see your opponent's next three moves. A lack of urgency and having a superiority complex about the work make these two imperatives, seeing the entire picture and long-term strategy, damn near impossible for creating a new world order.

Systems change is seen by them as "moving the chess pieces around the board" instead of intentionally wiping all those pieces off the board, turning the board over, and creating a revolution. This part right here, the revolution, terrifies the disability rights movement, well, honestly, the so-called progressive movement and damn near every white person in the world.

Brother Malcolm X said, "By any means necessary," and most of the time these words are presented with the image of him standing in front of a window peering through partially opened curtains being held open by his left hand while he holds an upright, fully loaded AK-40 rifle in his right hand. This is an iconic image that illustrates his complete readiness to protect his family and fight this war of oppression.

> We declare our right on this earth to be a man, to be a human being, to be respected as a human being, to be given the rights of a human being in this society, on this earth, in this day, which we intend to bring into existence by any means necessary.[5]

It is our inevitable right to fight for creating a new world order through disruption and protest. Changemakers around this globe know this to be true. The people are in the streets disrupting and laying down the foundation for the revolution in South Africa, Hong Kong, Paris, Brazil, Venezuela, Iran, Palestine, India, and on and on! Disorder is an essential part of revolt.

President Lyndon B. Johnson, a Democrat from Texas, did not wake up one morning in 1964 and say, "I think we should pass the Civil Rights Act and I am putting that on my agenda of things to get done this year." No, he woke up many days, along with millions of other Americans and people around the world, and watched those images of this country literally "on fire" from riots in multiple large inner cities. Black people put their lives on the line, telling him and all other powers that be, this is our "by any means necessary"!

To be the object of agitation is not a place that many people or organizations wish to find themselves. But as the saying goes, "With much power comes much responsibility." It is the duty of people who say they are creating change to hold power accountable. In the work of creating a new world order, the power of disruption is a necessity.

There are many congressional members who do not want to be confronted by the people, especially up close and personal in their DC congressional offices or in-state home offices. This is sometimes the only way to get the attention of members of Congress. I would not be a director of national policy creating, writing, and influencing policy in the halls of Congress and the White House without the thousands of powerful people who used (are using) their bodies, gave up what little safety they possessed, and went out on the streets of this country squared up and faced "The Man" and said ENOUGH!

CONCLUSION

arambee!

If you know me then you know that I am passionate about the work of creating a new world where there is an end to violence, racism, and all systems of oppression. But I am also stubborn as hell and hell-bent on making things happen. This strength comes from something spiritual inside me that I identified and cultivated at a young age and that pushes me to move forward. It was built on the foundation of the social justice campaigns, including making Dr. Martin Luther King Jr.'s birthday a national holiday. I was in eighth grade and a bunch of old white men in Congress told us that this will never be a federal holiday. Today there is not only a national holiday in his honor, but there is a national monument of this remarkable Black man on the United States National Mall. The other social justice campaign was dismantling South African apartheid and freeing Nelson Mandela when they told us he would die in prison, and that did not happen.

My drive comes from the complete belief of hope and the blessings of having learned from activists like Amiri Baraka, Sonia Sanchez, and my late fierce mother, Lillian Baldwin who taught me that when there are obstacles in the way, don't get angry, get organized. In that organizing call on the ancestors, use their logic and strategy and mirror your enemies' ruthlessness and fierceness to obtain victory by any means necessary.

In order to address trauma and agony inflicted upon people there must be purposeful reparations. Because where there has been harm, it has been proven over and over again that none of the parties involved will move forward to healing without atonement. The process of healing these terrible injustices to people of color and multi-marginalized communities currently functioning in the disability rights movement will never materialize until there is authentic and intentional penance by those committing, empowering, and ignoring the harm and those who are harmful.

Do disabled Black and Brown people and multi-marginalized communities want to reconcile with the dominant white disability rights movement? If the answer is yes, what does this look like? How is it measured for success? How is it sustained?

In the past couple of years, a number of Black and Brown and multi-marginalized disabled youth have asked me if I think that it is possible to have an accord in the disability rights movement. It is sad to report that my resolute answer to them was (and is) "no"—"absolutely not." There will be no harmony in this community until there is honest and deliberate work to first acknowledge there are huge problems like racism, misogynoir, elitism, xenophobia, supremacy, homophobia, and so much more rampant in this community. Then there must be a "truth and reparation" process with a clear strategy of the vision for progress.

The "players" who are leading the disability rights movement in the DC Beltway and around this country are in no way prepared to acknowledge this truth and most definitely have no desire to engage in creating change. The many pages prior to this section of the book are my truth in this work.

They have yet to come to recognize their truth and continue to denounce mine.

One of the most imperative lessons I have learned in my many years of working in coalitions and collaboratively with multiple groups of people is that the solutions to the problems must come from those who have lived experience in disability and are directly impacted. There can be no work done that is not designed and implemented by the oppressed, and the oppressor needs to get up from the table and leave the experts to do the work. The problem in this movement and many progressive movements is thinking that the tyrants are only found in the opposition.

Activist and author Charlene Carruthers discusses this in her book *Unapologetic: A Black, Queer, and Feminist Mandate for Radical Movements.*

> However, in almost every sector of our movement, the voiceless and powerless struggle for room in a world dominated by systems that oppress us and people who don't want us to be free. . . . Views of liberal white folks help perpetuate this problem.[1]

The revolution of dismantling these racist systems of oppression within the disability rights movement and the progressive movement at large will embody disruption, disorder, and agitation. This work must not be entered into as something that is momentary but as something that will be enduring; lasting movement changes that uplift and empower collective liberation.

It is imperative that Black and Brown and multi-marginalized disabled people confront the fear of white disabled and nondisabled people who dominate the disability rights movement (all progressive movements). This is an actual fear white people have of being removed from their dominant space of power (white privilege), even in the work of progressive and social justice work.

In the case of disabled white people, this is the white privilege they do not acknowledge as existing in their movement. This is directly tied into the atrocious Hindu caste system discussed earlier in this book, as the oppressors sit in denial when it comes to the revolution demanding that they no longer hold ownership of the movement. As Winston Churchill, the prime minister of Great Britain during WWII in the fight against the rise of fascism in Europe, said, *"You cannot reason with a tiger when your head is in its mouth."* Yes, Churchill was a racist and problematic, but this quote is spot-on. Because in both of these movements, disability rights and ending caste apartheid, there is no genuine acknowledgement of wrongdoing or privilege by the oppressors. Yet the oppressed are expected to be courteous, wait, give it time, and be reasonable.

————

These are my recommendations that come from many conversations with disabled people of color and those from multi-marginalized communities who have lived experience as being disabled or are directly impacted. I believe that in the case of the larger disability rights movement, the autocrats who are the cisgender, upper-middle class, white women need to leave the room and reappear only if they are invited to return. But their ableism and complete disrespect of disabled people and specifically disabled people of color and multi-marginalized being leaders will never allow them to engage in this type of effort. This is their paternalism at work, something these authoritarians claim to be against as they destructively toil in civil rights for disabled people.

The white disabled leadership in this movement feel that they are an imperative part of the revolution. But this is a false assertion because they do not yet comprehend or accept a pluralistic, anti-racist systems change. Their complacency and denial of the overt and covert oppressive actions discussed throughout this prose provide a historical framework as to why this pronouncement is seen by many as truth. As Virginia Woolf said, *"If you do not tell the truth about yourself you cannot tell it about other people."*[2] When confronted by people who have asserted their trauma and hurt, the culprit does not get to decide that they did not cause harm.

It has been proven in restorative practice work that not only do the victims need to be healed but so do the oppressors. Remember the discussion on power and how it is used in this work through direct and great force. In this community there is harsh exercise of authority and power by the white dominant leaders. Those who participate in this tyrannical deliberation of oppression also need healing.

I am a true believer in humanity in all situations. This perspective will be imperative for any plans to create passage for the white majority in the disability rights movement to move forward to a place of solidarity.

———

I have three recommendations to create solidarity in the larger disability rights movement around the country and in Washington, DC.

Three recommendations for obtaining solidarity in the disability rights movement:

1. Truth and reparations: This must focus on healing multiple communities

2. Funding. Be genuine in the work, stop "the dance for finance," and stop mimicking and dominating the space
3. Believe in Black people: The creation of multiple national disability justice organizations led by and for disabled Black and Brown and multi-marginalized communities to build a movement that will disrupt the harmful systems of disability rights

TRUTH AND REPARATIONS

The first message to the white dominant disability rights movement is to stop harming Black and Brown and multi-marginalized disabled people.

The components of this will be to focus on both truth and reparations. Truth is done through conversation, research, and educating the community at large. Reparations are continuous compensation that will require all parties involved for resolution—the victims and the oppressors—but be clear that the victims are the center and leaders of this work.

The most common form of engaging in truth and reparations is to create a commission that provides mandates for the community and this should be done for this effort.

A truth commission, or a truth and reparations commission, is a commission tasked with discovering and revealing past wrongdoing by a government (or, depending on the circumstances, non-state actors also) in the hope of resolving conflict left over from the past. This type of work is formerly known as truth and reconciliation, but many fighting for Black liberation no longer want nor need reconciliation. But we are demanding reparations, so we have changed this to truth and reparations.

- One mandate should be to inform the world about what actually happens in the work of the disability rights movement (this book is one person's perspective and only touches on a portion of the subjugations).

- There should be a set limit of time for implementing the mandate for change (decided by those leading the work).
- There should be a clear and concise description of what is to be achieved, which hopefully are reconciliation and renewed relationships that are authentic and embrace mutual understanding and respect.
- The process for doing this should be decided on by the experts: BIPOC disabled people. But some ideas:
  - End the erasure of all others; address and record a true history of disability rights and in particular how Section 504 and the ADA were achieved—one that is inclusive of all people's contributions, not just white people's
  - Community events—a national tour of engagement with communities of BIPOC and multi-marginalized people at the center of and leading these conversations
  - Honor those BIPOC and multi-marginalized disabled people who are identified in the research for the true historical narrative, as well as those who are currently activists in the work
- Why is this important? The disability rights movement needs this to embrace a pluralistic approach to the social justice work that needs to be done to create systems changes and a new world order.

FUNDING

In Peter Kropotkin's review of solidarity, he states: "In the long run the practice of solidarity proves much more advantageous to the species than the development of individuals endowed with predatory inclinations."[3] This meaning of this second message to the dominant white disability rights movement community is twofold: one, stop being disingenuous by engaging in this imperative work with an expectation of reward (stop being opportunistic), and two, stop being mimics who dominate this space for funds with misrepresentation.

In the past few years, philanthropy has finally acknowledged and interacted with the disability rights movement. But as always in this work that connection has been dominated by the white nondisabled and disabled in the movement. They extract funds mirroring terminology and phrases that make philanthropy's ears perk up: "racial equity," "Intersectionality," "creating spaces of equality." Yet they have no actual plans for genuine engagement or for a movement to eliminate oppressive and racist systems.

These organizations continue to have boards, leadership, and staff composed of if not all then mostly white people who continue to whitewash the policy and issue area work, as proven when they host panels on implicit bias that are completely made up of white people as the experts.

There must also be a removal of funding to those identified as opportunists who see this work as career and professional climbing. This would be those people and organizations who have no history of creating, promoting, and/or engaging in eliminating the oppressive racist systems within the disability rights movement.

Philanthropy must engage in the hiring of disabled Black and Brown and multi-marginalized people within their organizations. These should be positions of leadership where this community would have decision-making as well as strategic planning power. They should also be positions that provide market value or better compensation, healthcare, and other benefits. They should be in line with the very policies many fight for every day: living wages, genuine life-work balance policies, and opportunities for career growth. Currently this is severely missing in the nonprofit industrial complex but especially in many disability rights organizations.

The boards of trustees or directors for these philanthropic organizations must also include disabled Black and Brown and multi-marginalized people. This inclusion must equate to more than one, two, or even three "token" members and staff. The days of checking a box to be in compliance by having "a token" ended with the election of a despot forty-fifth president of the United States. There is no time to play games as the revolution is upon us.

BELIEVE IN BLACK PEOPLE

The final recommendation is that there should be the creation of multiple national disability justice organizations that are led by and for disabled Black and Brown and multi-marginalized people. These organizations should center and encompass the 10 Principles of Disability Justice as discussed in the glossary section of this book and created by Sins Invalid. This assertion means that I technically, morally, and ethically should not write a strategic plan for what these organizations look like or how they function. But what I will suggest is that every philanthropic group in this country provide funding and step away from being dictatorial over the resources provided.

It would be nice to see a provision or rule that only Black and Brown and multi-marginalized disabled people be hired in all positions and make up 100 percent of the board of directors for the first twenty years of the established organizations. This way the very people who have caused so much harm and who feel they must dominate the movement will have absolutely no power in these newly formed disability justice organizations.

The disability justice organizations created should center those who have been erased, ignored, disrespected, disenfranchised, and marginalized. These are things that will agitate the system and make white-privilege people feel uncomfortable. But so be it! The time has been long overdue in the disability rights movement and, I would dare say, the progressive movement that white people not only be uncomfortable; they also need to be uprooted from their perches of privilege.

No one knows what the future holds. But I am hopeful and faithful because of the thousands of activists out there who are creating purposeful systemic change. We are living in some hard times where many have lost hope and faith. My desire is to be part of and continue to grow the communities who are pushing forward despite these challenges. This will be done through those brave and committed BIPOC disabled and multi-marginalized activists I encounter daily. They are doing this in trauma-free spaces with those who are closest to the problem leading us to the solutions that will bring us to a place of equity and love.

ACKNOWLEDGMENTS

This book was a labor of love and passion and it took a village to get it done. I start with thanking my Lord and savior for without my faith in God I would be nowhere in this world. It is an honor to be the child of Lillian Lula and James Baldwin and sister of Philip Baldwin for whom I give the utmost appreciation. My life is defined by "my girls," my lifelong friends, and for them I am beyond grateful—thank you Ericka Truesdale, Vicki Carlisle, Michelle Mauro, Kimberley Crockett, and Monica Findley. My DC crew who has been there through all of this: Llenda Jackson-Leslie, Anita Cozart, Jasmine Tyler, Breon Wells, Chris Scott, Henry Floyd Jr., and Bertram Lee. My mentors in life and policy Pam Muscara and Laura Murphy.

The writing process is not an easy one and I give thanks to those who were part of the journey, for without them this would only be a dream. Thank you to Wallace Truesdale Sr. for your guidance and counsel. In this process I had a writing doctor who is amazing in the work of editing me and for him I am honored and appreciative to Will Myers.

I am blessed to know a number of successful and poignant authors who are also activists and who guided me to writing. Thank you to all of them who took their time to give me guidance, make connections, read this book, and anything more they did. I will not list them for there are so many. To my Beacon family, Joanna Green and the entire team, thank you for this opportunity to create a piece of writing that will hopefully forever be a work of hope. It is an honor and wonderful privilege to be part of such a great group of Beacon writers.

The community who have been my rock in disability and social justice work and continue to support me in moving the work to a better place—thank you Anita Cameron, Stan Holbrook (R.I.P.), Nadia Fischer, Rosa Clemente, Yoshiko Dart, Allison Donald, Ryan Easterly, Allilsa Fernandez, Kassandra Frederique, Andrew Goodwin (R.I.P.), Keri Gray, Keith Jones, Cedric Lawson, Vania Leveille, Leroy Moore, Andrea Ritchie, Axel Santana, Justice Shorter, Robert Stephens, Ashley White and Kevin Powell, V (formerly known as Eve Ensler), Dave Zirin, Laura Flanders, Thenmozhi Soundararajan, Susan Swan, Heather Sachs, Carol Tyson, and Karin Korb.

In all of this I will of course leave someone out, so please forgive me.

This is but a piece of my life and my journey in the work of social justice. I am beyond excited to know what this work will do for my community and for the work of disability justice. Thank you to the reader for picking up this book and telling others to read and for the community that will create solidarity for change. I remain committed to creating a new world order, one where Black disabled people are the center of the work for Black liberation.

NOTES

INTRODUCTION

1. Martin Luther King Jr., *Where Do We Go From Here: Chaos or Community?* (orig. 1967; Boston: Beacon Press, 2010).
2. M. Zwick-Maitreyi et al., *Caste in the United States: A Survey of Caste Among South Asian Americans*, Equality Labs, 2018, p. 9.
3. Sins Invalid, "10 Principles of Disability Justice," September 17, 2016, https://www.sinsinvalid.org/blog/10-principles-of-disability-justice.

CHAPTER 1: BUILDING AN ACTIVIST

1. W. E. B. Du Bois, *The Souls of Black Folk* (orig. 1907; Oxford: Oxford University Press, 2007), 7.

CHAPTER 2: CREATING A POLICY MAKER

1. Charlene Carruthers, *Unapologetic: A Black, Queer, and Feminist Mandate for Radical Movements* (Boston: Beacon Press, 2018).

CHAPTER 3: KNOWLEDGE IS POWER

1. Michelle Alexander, *The New Jim Crow: Mass Incarceration in the Age of Colorblindness* (New York: New Press, 2012), 56.

CHAPTER 4: DIRECT WITH GREAT FORCE

1. Ida B. Wells, "Southern Horrors: Lynch Laws in All Its Phases," in *The Light of Truth: Writings of an Anti-Lynching Crusader* (New York: Penguin Classics, 2014).
2. Gore Vidal, "Robert Graves and the Twelve Caesars," in *Rocking the Boat* (New York: Dell, 1963), commenting on Graves's translation of Suetonius's *The Twelve Caesars* (orig. 1957; London: Penguin, 2007).
3. From Audre Lorde, *Sister Outsider: Essays and Speeches* (Berkeley, CA: Crossing Press, 1984).

4. "Olmstead: Community Integration for Everyone," Information and Technical Assistance on the Americans with Disabilities Act, https://archive.ada.gov/olmstead/olmstead_about.htm, accessed August 10, 2023.

5. Bruce Hartford, *The Selma Voting Rights Struggle and March to Montgomery* (San Francisco: Westwind Writers, 2014).

6. Thomas LaVeist and Lydia A. Isaac, eds., *Race, Ethnicity, and Health: A Public Health Reader* (New York: John Wiley & Sons, 2012).

7. Sarah Jones, "A Republican Congressman Compared the Americans with Disabilities Act to Jim Crow," *New Republic*, July 27, 2018.

8. Andrew Kaczynski et al., "GOP Congressman Said Blacks Have an 'Entitlement Mentality' and View Themselves as Victims," CNN Politics, July 21, 2018, https://edition.cnn.com/2018/07/20/politics/kfile-jason-lewis-racial-comments/index.html.

9. M. Zwick-Maitreyi et al., *Caste in the United States: A Survey of Caste Among South Asian Americans*, Equality Labs, 2018, p. 9.

10. Michelle Alexander, *New Jim Crow: Mass Incarceration in the Age of Colorblindness* (New York: New Press, 2012).

CHAPTER 5: DISABILITY IN THE BELTWAY

1. Robin DiAngelo, *White Fragility: Why It's So Hard for White People to Talk About Racism* (Boston: Beacon Press, 2018).

2. Roy Walmsley, "World Prison Population List," 8th ed., International Centre for Prison Studies, King's College, London, https://www.prisonpolicy.org/scans/wppl-8th_41.pdf, accessed September 18, 2023.

3. Martin Luther King Jr., *Strength to Love* (orig. 1963; Boston: Beacon Press, 2019).

4. DiAngelo, *White Fragility*.

5. 1964 speech. In Malcolm X and Simon Starr, *The Bullet or the Ballot* (Scotts Valley, CA: CreateSpace, 2018).

CONCLUSION

1. Charlene Carruthers, *Unapologetic: A Black, Queer, and Feminist Mandate for Radical Movements* (Boston: Beacon Press, 2018).

2. Virginia Woolf, "The Leaning Tower," *The Essays of Virginia Woolf*, Vol. 6; *1933 to 1941*, ed. Stuart N. Clarke (London: Chatto and Windus, 2011), 274, noted in http://www.virginiawoolfsociety.org.uk/resources/misquotations.

3. Peter Kropotkin, *Mutual Aid: A Factor of Evolution* (1891; London: Freedom Press, 1987).